Dedication:

This book is for all those people who feel like they're stuck in one place going nowhere. Maybe you don't have a mother or a father and you share a car with a friend or sibling to get to work. Things will change!

Sometimes, a golden opportunity plops right in your lap. You might not see it at the time because of stress and the fog of other problems but it's there. It's up to you to see through the mess of life and seize that moment.

The most important changes in life do not come without some sacrifice and maybe a dash of embarrassment. If you find your calling, go for it. You just have to believe in yourself.

Olivia:

The Queen Bee

By Frank James Bailey

PROLOGUE

OLIVIA

The world is full of wrestlers who want to be famous like Hulk Hogan, Jake the Snake Roberts, Chyna, Asuka, or Misty Blue

Very few will reach this status.

My name is Olivia Lenna. Better known as Olivia: The Mighty Kraken. This is the story on how I became the greatest female wrestler in the world without selling my soul to be super famous.

Chapter 1

JAXON

Most of you have seen that nineties movie called Jerry Maguire. It's about a sports agent who gets fired and then he only has one client the entire movie. His livelihood depended on one football player getting a new contract so he could make his cut.

Well, I'm like that guy. My name is Jaxon Anderson and I work at an agency called Westman Sports Agency in Indianapolis, Indiana. We're in the Midwest so with two hundred plus agencies all over the world we're around number one hundred fifty. We're not on the bottom but we're nowhere near the top of the list. There is a lot of competition out there and we're all after the top athletes.

As an agent my job is to find the talent, get them a good deal and make sure they make the agency money. They perform, do shows, and sign autographs and maybe do a commercial or two. I get my cut and the agency gets their cut too.

Most of the time things work out great. Other times, not so much. There are sports injuries and some athletes are very difficult to work with. You know, just like that movie.

I deal in all sports but mostly female wrestling. That's my division and it's the sport I know the most about. It's the fastest growing sport in America and there are so many groups and leagues I can sign a lady up with. The top ones are WOW (Women of Wrestling), ECW (Extreme Championship Wrestling), WWE (World Wrestling Entertainment), and AWWL (American Women's Wrestling League). If they have the talent, the drive, and the body to handle the abuse from being banged around we can all make good money.

On occasion, I have to manage a few wrestlers on top of signing them but most of the time I find the talent, sign them and then they're on their own to find a manager.

Today marked my three-year anniversary at Westman and I still feel like I'm still at the bottom. The girls I've signed are all small-time athletes and another work associate, who I can't stand, stole a few clients from me. Even with all that, I love what I do and I don't want to quit. I've made the company money and I've made money too, but I have a feeling I can do more. Like I'm destined for something bigger.

That's enough about what I do. Moving on.

Ever have one of those days where everything goes wrong, an unbelievably dreadful day? April 25 was that day for me. I will never forget it because I didn't know it at the time but that's the day the dominos started to fall.

The faint hum of the evening greeted me as I stepped through the front door, the weight of the day still clinging to my shoulders. The air inside was warm, carrying the rich, savory aroma of garlic, soy sauce, and ginger. My stomach growled in response, and I felt the tension in my chest loosen just a little. Noa stood in the kitchen, her back to me, her dark hair tied up in a loose bun. She turned, her face lighting up with that smile that always made the world feel lighter.

"Hi, honey," she said, her voice soft but carrying that warmth that felt like home.

"Hey," I replied, shrugging off my jacket and hanging it by the door. The scent of the stir-fry was intoxicating, and I couldn't help but grin. "It amazes me how you always have dinner ready the second I walk in. Do you have a sixth sense or something?"

She laughed, a sound that felt like sunlight breaking through clouds. "Maybe I just know you too well. Go sit down. It's almost ready."

I wandered into the dining room, where the table was set with two plates—one piled high with chicken stir-fry for me, the other with a colorful vegetable medley for her. The steam rising from the food carried the scent of sesame oil and chili, and my mouth watered. I sat down, my fingers drumming lightly on the table as I waited for her to join me.

Noa slid into her seat across from me, her eyes searching mine. "How was work?" she asked, her tone gentle but probing.

I hesitated, poking at my food with my fork. "Not great," I admitted. "Heather's retiring early. Her injury's worse than we thought."

Noa's brow furrowed. "I thought she got hurt in the ring?"

"She did," I said, taking a bite of the stir-fry. The flavors exploded on my tongue—sweet, salty, and just the right amount of heat. "But apparently something else happened that made it worse. Now she's getting a divorce too. Wants to focus on being a better mom."

Noa nodded slowly, her chopsticks hovering over her plate. "Wasn't she married to that wrestler... what's his name? Mike something?"

"'The Mad Dog,'" I supplied. "Mike 'The Mad Dog.' They've got a daughter, Becca." I paused, my chest tightening as I thought about us, about the empty nursery we'd painted last year, the doctor's words still echoing in my head. *Practically shooting blanks.* I set my fork down, my appetite suddenly waning.

Noa noticed, her gaze softening. "What's wrong?"

I sighed, running a hand through my hair. "I just... I want a family with you, Noa. We've tried and tried, but..."

She reached across the table, her fingers brushing against mine. "Trying is fun," she said, her voice teasing but gentle.

I managed a small smile. "I'm not complaining about that part."

She squeezed my hand. "Jaxon, you're twenty-five. We've got time. If the universe wants us to have kids, it'll happen."

I looked away, my jaw tightening. Noa's faith in the universe, in karma and balance, was something I admired but couldn't fully embrace. "The universe or not, the doctors said it's not happening for me. I'm... I'm not exactly fertile ground here."

Her expression didn't falter. "I don't like seeing you sad," she said softly. "Let's talk about something else."

I took a long drink of water, trying to push the thoughts aside. "How's the gym?" I asked, forcing a lighter tone.

"Same as always," she said, picking up her chopsticks again. "Eric's still running it, and I pop in to make sure everything's smooth. Your wrestlers keep coming, though. Heather loved it there."

"Yeah," I said, forcing a smile. "You've been great for business. That discount you gave us didn't hurt either."

We fell into a comfortable silence for a while, the clink of utensils against plates the only sound.

Just as I was starting to relax, my phone buzzed on the table. I glanced at the screen—Flora Howard. My stomach sank. Flora was one of my clients, and she wasn't exactly known for good timing.

I answered the video call, trying to keep the irritation out of my voice. "Flora. What's the emergency?"

Her face filled the screen, her expression defiant. "There's no emergency."

"Then why are you calling me at home after hours?" I asked, my tone sharper than I intended.

"I'm leaving Westman," she said bluntly.

I blinked, caught off guard. "What? Why?"

"Mostly because of you."

I felt a flash of anger but forced myself to stay calm. "What did I do?"

"It's not what you did, Jaxon. It's what you didn't do. I've been with Westman for over a year, and I still haven't gotten my shot at a title."

I took a deep breath, remembering Noa's advice about keeping my temper in check. "Flora, you're not ready. Being great takes time. You're not a superstar yet."

Her eyes narrowed. "Yet? I should be! I train four days a week. I've put in the work. I deserve more."

"You're not ready," I repeated, my voice firm. "You think you are, but—"

She cut me off. "I talked to Toni at the AWWL. She thinks I'm wasting my time with you. She wants to rebrand me."

I clenched my fist under the table, my nails digging into my palm. "The AWWL? That's a celebrity circus, Flora. You're better than that."

"Exactly!" she snapped. "I should be one of those celebrities. Getting deals, making money. I don't have any of that here."

I exhaled slowly, trying to keep my voice steady. "Come into the office on Monday. We'll talk about rebranding."

"No," she said, her tone final. "My contract's up. I'm done."

The call ended, and I stared at the blank screen, my jaw clenched so tight it hurt. Noa's hand on my arm pulled me back to the present.

"Jaxon," she said softly. "It's okay. You've still got other clients and we've got the wedding coming up. You can take some time to figure things out."

I shook my head, frustration bubbling up. "Noa, Heather and Flora were my biggest earners. Without them, I don't know how I'm going to keep up with everything."

She smiled, her calm unwavering. "You'll figure it out. You always do. If you need to, you can always come work at the gym."

I groaned, running a hand over my face. "I don't want to rely on your business to support us. I need to bring in money too."

"Then find new clients," she said simply. "Or find that one big client who'll change everything. The universe has a way of providing, Jaxon. You just have to be open to it."

I chuckled despite myself. "You and your universe."

She leaned in, her eyes sparkling. "Don't forget—less is more. Focus on what you can do for your clients, not what they can do for you."

I sighed, leaning back in my chair. "I'll try. Right now, less is all I've got."

Noa reached for my hand again, her touch grounding me. "It's going to be okay. Hey, at least you've got your bachelor party to look forward to."

I groaned again, this time with a hint of a smile. "Yeah, about that. My friends want to take me somewhere 'surprising.' Why can't we just go fishing or to a game?"

She laughed, the sound like music. "Because it's a bachelor party, Jaxon. It's supposed to be fun. Let loose a little."

I rolled my eyes but couldn't help smiling. "Fine, but if there are naked dancing girls, I'm blaming you."

She kissed me, her lips soft and reassuring. "You're such a goofball. I trust you. Just have fun."

As she pulled away, I felt a little of the weight lift from my shoulders. Noa had a way of doing that—of reminding me that even when things felt impossible, there was always a way forward. Even if I didn't always believe in her "universe," I believed in her.

As we were almost done with dinner she asked, "If it will make you feel better, we can meditate on it."

"Does it have to be meditation, or can I suggest something else?"

She gave me a sweet stare, "That comes after meditation sweetie."

Chapter 2

OLIVIA

I'm going to get straight to the point because that's who I am. I don't like it when people take forever to tell me something.

My name is Olivia Lenna, I'm twenty-four and I'm very tall. I've been tall most of my life. With my wavy brown hair and brown eyes, I think I'm either Italian or Greek. My mom never told me much about my nationality. I asked but she never gave me a straight answer.

I don't know anything about my biological father because he ran out on my mom before I was born. She found a man just before my first birthday, he's the one I called dad.

When I was eight, I was five feet ten. Taller than everyone in the third grade. By the time I was thirteen, I grew to six feet tall, I was the tallest person in my class. Taller than all the boys. How many thirteen-year-old girls do you know that are six feet tall? I assume not many.

By the time I was fifteen I grew to my maximum height of six feet six inches. I always hovered around two hundred pounds. My body wasn't full of muscles or very tone at the time but I wasn't fat by any means. Thank God I stopped growing when I was a teenager. Finding clothes to fit a woman my height was not easy. Most of the time I had to shop in the big and tall men's stores.

You might think with my massive height I would have played basketball in high school. Nope! I never did. As a matter of fact, I've never been much into sports, but I did play volleyball for fun and wrestled a little bit too. Nothing serious.

Wherever I went, no matter what I did, my height always gave me more attention than I could handle.

When I was younger, I did my best to avoid attention, which was hard to do. Now that I'm a little older I use my height and my large stature to my advantage when I can. It's a part of me. I've learned to accept it.

The only person I ever called dad was Mike. He was actually Emma's dad. She's my younger sister. More on her in a bit. Mike was a seriously strict father. When my sister and I were just kids I remember he drank a lot. Two cases of beer a week. He was in and out of jobs a lot. Some of them he quit, with others he was let go. Life was hard for him and he took it out on his family.

When Emma and I were kids, Mike would beat my little sister and me with the belt for not doing what he demanded of us. Not doing our chores, yard work and getting bad grades in school were just a few excuses he used.

When I grew taller than him, he didn't yell at me as much as he used to, except for when he was drunk and felt like he had more courage. However, he always screamed at my little sister because she wasn't turning out the way he wanted.

Speaking of my sister, Emma is a very naive nineteen-year-old. She's short. Well, everyone is short to me. She's five feet six, red hair, hazel eyes, very skinny and very pretty. She loves to party, have fun and sleep around a lot. A lifestyle I very much disagree with but she's my sister and I tend to look after her when I can.

When Emma was a toddler, she would repeat movements a lot which drove my dad crazy. I didn't think anything of it. Kids are kids.

Emma also hated the fireworks on the Fourth of July when she was little too. They were too noisy. On occasion my dad would call her name and she didn't respond. It pissed him off when she ignored him so he would hit her with the belt for not listening. He was a mean dad.

When Emma was sixteen, right after she got her driver's license, our dad died in a horrible car accident. She's been a wild one ever since. I think she's been hiding her feelings behind her lifestyle.

My mom Joyce always seemed to protect Emma more than me. She hugged her more, gave her more attention and on more than one occasion, tried to stop her husband from beating Emma with the belt.

Maybe it was because I grew so fast that dad didn't bother me as much once I towered over him.

Despite Emma's zest for life, she's an exceptionally good artist. Ever since she was a little girl, she's always loved to draw. She was going to go to a special art class before our dad died. After that tragic day she never really gave art a chance.

I don't have an artistic bone in my body. We are definitely not alike.

After he died, mom took care of us, on her own, until last year. As far as I know my mom never did drugs. She tried her best to take care of two kids all by herself.

Right after Emma graduated high school, on a Tuesday, she met someone about a delivery job. This person set her up.

She did everything she could to explain to the judge that she was set up. They never found this other person so she couldn't prove she was doing a job for someone. She also had a bad public defender too. All they saw was a chance to get a drug dealer off the streets. I was her only family in the court room when my mom got a five-year prison sentence.

I could hear her crying as they took her away. It tore me up to.

So, let's add this up. No mom and no dad. We do have an aunt who is deeply religious. Her name is Karen. Very fitting for her attitude toward us. She doesn't like the way Emma is living her life and she always considered me a freak of nature. I remember she told my mom once that I should get my height reduced. No female should be that tall. As if my height is something that could be fixed.

She avoids us as much as possible which is fine by me. With no other relatives to turn to, my sister and I share an apartment together.

The apartment was small, but it was ours. The faint hum of the refrigerator buzzed in the background, and the smell of cheap coffee lingered in the air. I'd just come back from another delivery gig in my dad's old pickup truck, my shoulders aching from hauling furniture all day. At 6'1", I didn't exactly blend in, and most places didn't want to hire someone who looked like they could bench-press their manager. But I made it work. We had to.

Emma burst through the door, her cheeks flushed and her eyes bright with excitement. She dropped her Wal-Mart vest on the couch like it was a dead weight she'd been carrying for years. "Olivia, you won't believe it!" she said, her voice bubbling over. "I met this guy today—Frank. He told me about this place I could work at. Like, *real* money."

I paused, the half-empty water bottle in my hand freezing mid-air. "Some guy named Frank? What kind of place are we talking about?"

She grinned, her teeth flashing. "A bar. Well, not just a bar. A *gentleman's club*. It's called The Rat Hole. Isn't that cool?"

The name hit me like a punch to the gut. "The Rat Hole? Emma, that sounds like the kind of place where people go to disappear."

She rolled her eyes, her excitement undeterred. "Oh, come on. It's just a name. Frank said I could make way more than I do at Wal-Mart. Like, hundreds in a night."

I set the water bottle down, my palms pressing into the edge of the counter. "Emma, you're not even twenty. You can't just—"

"Frank said he'd get me a fake ID," she interrupted, waving her hand like it was no big deal. "Says I'll pass for twenty-one easy."

"No. Absolutely not." My voice came out sharper than I meant it to, but the thought of her in a place like that made my stomach churn. "Do you even hear yourself? A fake ID? A strip club? Mom would kill me if she knew I let you do something like that."

Her face darkened, and she crossed her arms over her chest. "You're not my mom, Olivia. You don't get to tell me what to do."

The words stung, but I didn't let it show. "You're right. I'm not Mom. But Mom's in prison, and that means I'm the one who has to look out for you. And I'm not going to let you throw yourself into some sketchy place just because some guy named Frank said it's a good idea."

She glared at me, her jaw tightening. "You don't get it. I'm tired of scraping by, Olivia. I'm tired of wearing this stupid vest and dealing with customers who treat me like crap. This is my chance to actually make something of myself."

"Make something of yourself?" I shot back, my voice rising. "By taking your clothes off for strangers? Emma, that's not a life. That's a trap."

She didn't answer. Instead, she grabbed her bag and stormed out, slamming the door so hard the walls shook. I stood there, my hands clenched into fists, the sound of her footsteps fading down the hallway. The apartment felt suddenly too quiet, too empty.

I should've gone after her. I should've found Frank and put the fear of God into him. Maybe even called the cops. But I didn't. Because as much as I wanted to protect her, I knew pushing too hard would only drive her further away. And I couldn't lose her. Not like this.

The Rat Hole. Just the name made my skin crawl. I'd been in enough dive bars and back-alley joints to know what kind of place it was—dim lights, sticky floors, and men who thought they owned the world. Emma didn't belong there. She was too young, too stubborn, too… *Emma*. But she was also desperate, and desperation made people do stupid things.

I sank onto the couch, the weight of the day pressing down on me. The smell of her cheap perfume still lingered in the air, a reminder of how close she was—and how far away she felt. I didn't know how to fix this. I didn't know how to be the person she needed me to be. All I knew was that I couldn't let her go down this path alone.

Against my better judgment, I allowed her to work there, only to discover that the place was a bizarre fusion of history and hedonism—an underground bunker repurposed into a clandestine strip bar.

This wasn't just any bar; it was a literal hole in the earth. The space, once a doomsday bomb shelter, now pulsed with neon lights and thrumming bass, its thick concrete walls absorbing the energy of the night. I couldn't help but worry about the ventilation, imagining the stale air trapped beneath the weight of the earth. Yet, to my surprise, the air remained relatively fresh, even with the occasional haze of cigarette smoke curling through the shadows.

Despite my reservations, I had to admit—there was a strange, almost eerie charm to the place. The raw, industrial aesthetic of the bunker, paired with the flickering glow of red and blue lights, gave it an edgy, underground allure that felt both dangerous and irresistible.

Emma used the stage name Trixie.

One of my biggest mistakes in life was letting her get that fake ID and work at that bar.

In her first week, only working a few days, she made over fifteen hundred dollars. That's double what she made at Wal-Mart in a full week.

As her big sister, I felt it was my job to look out for her. So, when she started working at The Rat Hole, I did what any overprotective sibling would do: I got a job there too. Well, technically, Emma got me the job. For a few weeks, I was juggling two jobs—deliveries during the day and bouncing at night.

I wasn't stacked with muscles, but I didn't need to be. At six-foot-six, I was a force of nature. My height alone was enough to make most people think twice before crossing me. I had this way of standing—shoulders back, chin up—that made me seem even taller, like I was carved out of some unshakable mountain.

Let me be clear: I don't strip. I'm the bouncer. In a place like The Rat Hole, that's a job that requires more brains than brawn, though a little intimidation never hurts.

I wasn't jacked, but I wasn't a skinny rail either. Years of hauling deliveries in and out of my truck had given me a solid build, and my height did the rest. People tend to rethink their life choices when someone my size looms over them.

My job was simple: stand at the door, keep an eye on the crowd, and make sure no one got too handsy with the dancers. Most nights were uneventful, but every now and then, someone decided to test their luck.

One night, a few weeks into the job, I spotted trouble brewing at a corner table. A drunk guy in a cowboy hat—let's call him Tex—was getting a little too friendly with Coco. I watched as his hand wandered where it shouldn't, and when Trixie walked by, he grabbed her too. That was my cue. I walked over, my military boots thudding against the sticky floor, and leaned down to his level.

"Hey, Tex," I said, my voice calm but firm. "Did you just grab Coco's boob?"

He smirked, his breath reeking of cheap beer. "Yeah, so? It's a fucking strip club. What's the big deal? By the way, the name's Bob, not Tex."

I straightened up, towering over him. "Well, Bob, the big deal is you also harassed Trixie. Strip club or not, she's family."

He glanced at his buddy and let out a drunken laugh. "Dude, a two-for-one! Maybe they'll cum kiss, snowball, and let me watch."

That was it. I took a deep breath, my patience officially spent. "You and your buddy are going to have to leave. Now."

He sneered, his face red with alcohol and arrogance. "Why? Our money's good here."

I didn't waste time arguing. In one swift motion, I yanked him out of his seat by the collar of his shirt. He flailed like a ragdoll, his cowboy hat tumbling to the floor. "Leave. Now. Before I throw you out the hard way."

He didn't like that. As I started dragging him toward the door, he swung a wild punch at me, screaming, "You bitch!"

I caught his fist mid-air like it was a slow-pitch softball, my fingers wrapping around his knuckles with ease. I twisted his arm behind his back and kept moving, his buddy trailing behind like a scared puppy. The guy didn't even try to help—just stood there, wide-eyed and silent.

Frank, the owner, watched from behind the bar, a smirk tugging at his lips. At the time, I thought he was just pleased with how I handled the situation. Now, I know better. Frank's mind worked in ways I didn't want to understand.

I shoved Bob out the door, and he landed face-first in the muddy parking lot, the rain pouring down on him like nature's own punishment. He groaned, trying to push himself up, but I wasn't done. I leaned in the doorway, my arms crossed, and called out, "Bob?"

He looked up, his face a mix of anger and humiliation. "What?"

I smirked, my tone dripping with sarcasm. "Just remember—I didn't hit you. I only threw you out. If I'd punched you, they'd be calling an ambulance right now."

He didn't say a word. He just scrambled to his feet, his buddy helping him stumble toward their truck. I watched them go, the rain soaking my shirt, and felt a small surge of satisfaction. Another night, another idiot dealt with. Just another day in the life of The Rat Hole's resident giant.

After that incident, I got a reputation. Don't mess with the tall female bouncer, she'll kick your ass. Most of the time, if dudes saw a towering woman standing guard at the front door or walking around, they were likely to behave.

It wasn't too long after that altercation I quit making deliveries and made bouncing for Frank my full-time job. I made a hundred and fifty dollars a night, sometimes more. If the girls needed extra protection, they'd give me a tip too.

On occasion, when I would go into the dressing room, before Emma went on stage to dance, I noticed she would sketch drawings on napkins.

From simple flowers, to trees, to people too. Her attention to detail was unbelievable for a simple sketch.

Like I said, Emma is incredibly good at drawing art but in her eyes, art didn't make any money, stripping did.

Chapter 3

OLIVIA

I hadn't visited my mom in prison for a while. When she was first locked up, I would visit her about once a week. That slowly changed to once a month and later that schedule faded after I became a bouncer.

My visits might have slacked off because my mom was rather difficult to deal with. Every mother will claim to not favor one particular child, but we all know that moms lie, sometimes.

I needed to visit her from time to time to let her know what was going on with her kids. Sadly, every time I took the time to visit her it never went well.

On Memorial Day weekend, since I had that Monday off, I walked into the visiting area of the jail, but she didn't seem too excited to see me.

I waited in the cubical as the guard called her out, "Joyce Lenna, you have a visitor. Booth 5."

My eyes watched as she walked over to the booth. Growing up she had red hair like my sister but today the redness has faded. A few gray hairs fell in front of her face, but she didn't seem to care. My mother and I had the same nose and chin but everything else about her was a match for my sister.

Then I picked up my phone on the wall, "Hi mom."

She looked rough through the glass window. Her thinning red hair looked like a rat's nest and her face seemed to exude depression mixed with frustration.

She picked up her end, "Hi Olivia. It's been months and you finally came to see your mother? What took you so long?"

"I'm sorry I haven't come by. I was busy with my new job."

"How is my little girl?"

There it is. Her favorite child. I just told her I have a new job and she wants to know about Emma. My mom always did like her best, "How's your little girl? Didn't you hear me? I got a new job."

"I know. Heard you. How's Emma??"

She frustrated me so much. I lightly gritted my teeth as I said, "Mom, dad died when I was twenty."

"Emma's dad."

"Really mom?"

"I'm just sayin'"

Irritated I continued, "Anyway, not too long after that you went to prison for dealing drugs. How do you think your kids are doing?"

"I know you can take care of yourself. You're a big tough girl. Now how's Emma doing?"

I sighed, "As I told you the last time I visited, after you came…well, here – we got an apartment together. What you don't know is Emma got a job as a stripper at this gentleman's club named The Rat Hole."

"A gentleman's club? The Rat Hole? What the fuck, Olivia! You let her work there. She's only nineteen!"

I was growing frustrated with her, "That's right. She's nineteen, mom. She's at that age where she can do anything she wants."

"Why didn't you stop her?"

Is this woman even listening to a word I say? "Don't worry mom. I got a job there too. As the bouncer. I did that to keep an eye on her."

"Still, my baby shouldn't be working as a prostitute."

A prostitute? Seriously? I told her, "She's not a hooker mom. She's a dancer. She dances and takes her clothes off for anyone who…"

"I know what a stripper is. I'm just surprised you let her get a job there. Everyone knows that most of those places are shady. Men go there for sex in the back rooms."

As she talked, I rolled my eyes. "It's possible but I'm the bouncer remember. If I saw something like that, I'd put a stop to it."

"I'm just sayin.' Emma needs guidance. Sometimes she gets fixated…"

I put my hand under my chin to keep myself listening because my brain wasn't, "Again mom, she's old enough to do what she wants."

This conversation was going nowhere. I was done with her, "You know what, mom? Never mind. I'm out of here."

I hung up my phone and I could just barely hear her from the other side of the window. "Why are you leaving so soon? You need to get Emma out of that bar. You hear me?"

I didn't hear anymore after that. I left the room.

Chapter 4

JOYCE

Not too long after Olivia paid me a visit, it was time for my first parole hearing. It had been eighteen months since I was sentenced to five-years in prison for dealing drugs.

I was going to tell Olivia about this court date, but I was so distracted by her letting my baby work at a strip club I completely forgot to tell her about it before she ran off.

This hearing was not like the last time when I was in court and sentenced. This was a video call. I assume it was because this was cheaper than dragging me out of my cell, putting me on a bus and hiring guards to escort me to a court. Money is always the biggest factor when it comes to this crap.

I was led into a small room by a prison guard. This room smelled funkier than a three-day old unwashed sock because of all the other prisoners brought in here.

My public defender was also on the call too. He was in his office or at home.

What upset me was, this was my first parole hearing, and I never left the prison. It's like they didn't even care.

The judge said in the video conference call, "Good afternoon, Mrs. Lenna."

"Good afternoon to you to your honor."

This man looked like he was in his nineties. I'm sure he wasn't that old. He reminded me of Mitch McConnell. An old white guy who doesn't really care about people. He told me, "My name is the Honorable Judge John Beckensmith. This is my last parole hearing of the day so let's make this quick. Mr. Goodwin, you'll be defending Joyce in this hearing?"

"Yes, your honor."

I felt betrayed. This was my attorney? I've never met him before in my life.

The judge said, "Joyce, you're currently serving a five-year sentence for a level five felony drug trafficking charge. Tell me in your own words why I should release you to the public after only eighteen months."

"Your honor, my daughter Emma needs me. She's only nineteen. My sister Karen, who lives an hour south of Indy, never responds to my calls or emails so my little girl is on her own."

"You're daughter Emma. You say she's nineteen? So, she's out of high school then?"

"Yes. But I think she's…"

"Does Emma have anyone to take care of her."

"Well, yes. She's living with someone."

"She's nineteen and living with someone? It sounds to me like Emma is an adult now. Paying her own bills and living with a roommate."

"Well, yes but Emma needs help. My help. A mothers help."

The judge asked my attorney, "Mr. Goodwin, Did you know about Emma?"

"Yes, when this case started, she was seventeen."

"And now she's nineteen?"

"Correct."

Pleading with him I said, "Your honor. She tends to get hyper focused on stuff. The wrong stuff. I just found out she's working in a…"

He stopped me, "She's old enough to be on her own. I think she'll be fine while you're serving your sentence."

I tried to reason with him, "No, she won't. Listen…"

"Mr. Goodwin, do you have anything to add on her behalf?"

My lame ass attorney did very little to defend me, "No, nothing to add at this time, your honor."

"Joyce, I don't feel that you've changed at all since you were sentenced."

I heard the gavel slam down.

"Parole is denied."

I tried desperately to say something, "Wait. That's it? That was way too fast. You're honor I…"

The video feed ended, and I never got a chance to finish. It looks like all he wanted to do was get my case to be over with as soon as possible so he could leave for the day.

I shook my fist at the TV and screamed, "AAhhhh!"

A guard named Pam Conners saw how disappointed I was. She told me, "Come on. Time to go." She cuffed my hands to my belt and off we went.

Pam was the one guard that has known me since day one.

This simple walk back to my cell usually took five minutes or less but today it seemed like an eternity. All I wanted was for someone to listen to me.

As tears rolled down my face, Pam walked me back to my cell. She asked, "Rough day?"

I didn't respond. My cries told her everything she needed to know.

I felt like nobody was listening to me. Olivia didn't listen to me when I told her to get Emma out of the strip bar and now this judge didn't pay any attention to me either.

I hope I can get out of here soon to take care of my little girl.

Chapter 5

FRANK

I adjusted my Sony handheld video camcorder and moved it a little on my desk to get the perfect view. Then I looked down for just a moment and then looked up at my camera again. "Am I recording? It looks like it. Okay, here we go. This is a little mini movie I'm making for…er, well, anyone. Especially me."

I closed my eyes, turned the view finder around and realized the recording had stopped. So, I hit record again, "I'm terrible at this shit but…anyway, here we go. Real start this time, three, two, one." I took a deep breath and said, "How you doin? I'm Frank Gambini. I'm forty-eight years old and I'm making a little mini movie today. I'm no big time Hollywood producer or anything like that but this is my first test run video."

I opened a drawer and pulled out some stationery, then looked back at the camera, pointing to the logo on the paper. "You see this? This is my club. I'm the owner of the Rat Hole. It sounds like a bad name for a bar, but I wanted it that way. The whole point of that crazy name was to discourage the wrong kind of people from coming to the bar. Unless you knew what kind of place this was, would you want to come to a bar called The Rat Hole? Yeah, I didn't think so."

Putting the paper down, I continued, "The Rat Hole is actually a gentleman's club in Pittsburg, Indiana. This town is in the middle of fuckin nowhere. I bought the property in an auction for cheap, found out the previous owner was a doomsday nut and he built an underground fallout shelter.

This shelter was massive. I gutted it out, added more ventilation and turned it into what it is now."

I smiled and thought, "I love my life. As I sit here in my office of the bar I own, let me tell you about me."

I looked away from my camera, toward my office door for just a second then back at my camera, "In case you can't tell by my thick dark mustache, slicked back black hair and a few gold chains, I'm Italian. My unique look sets me apart from the clientele who come to my bar. It's an Italian thing. Capiche?"

I took a promotional flyer out of my drawer and pointed to it, "I love this place, since it's deep underground and we're surrounded by thick concrete walls, it's a dead zone for cell reception. No cell phone reception means nobody can do that stupid live streaming shit that the kids do today. There's only one phone in the bar that anyone can use. The original lane line that I had turned back on. The twenty something kids are amazed it still works."

I moved the camera, just a pinch to get a better background view and continued, "I've owned this establishment for over two years, and I've never advertised on the internet or TV. This place has become popular by word of mouth. The bars reputation has spread that this 'men's club' is unique. Generous portions of food, strong drinks but they mostly come here for the entertainment."

"Guys come to The Rat Hole because it's legendary, and the girls can make great money too."

I smirked before I continued recording, "If you're thinking that the cops are going to close me down well, you'd be wrong."

"Not only is it hard to find but my nephew Tommy DeBrono is the sheriff in this county so I can get away with a lot more illegal stuff. Kinda like that 80's movie Porky's."

I looked at my laptop computer on my desk and checked the time, "She's late."

Then I looked back at my video, "Where was I? Oh yeah. Let me tell you how the inside is laid out. I know I could easily point the camera around the bar, but I have a meeting starting soon so for now, let me tell you."

"There are three stages in the bar. Two smaller stages and one big stage. The main stage gets most of the attention and that's where most of the customers gather, which means the girls can make the most money on the main stage. We even have a few private rooms for private lap dances. Those are extra."

I heard a knock on my office door. Before I let them in, I said in my video, "Being the entrepreneur that I am, I use all this info to my advantage." Then I answered my door, "Come on in."

Walking in my office was a beautiful looking redhead in her early twenties. Perfect body, thirty-eight double 'D' boobs, thin stomach, and a nice round bootie. Her lips were full, plump, and as sweet looking like a fresh strawberry.

She was wearing a very tight red bikini that was two sizes too small. It made her cleavage look like the Grand Canyon. I told her, "You're late."

She answered with a playful pouty look, "I'm sorry. I took a shower and didn't dry off, as you requested."

"I do love how you're all wet and shiny. You look so amazing. I'll forgive you, this time."

Kim closed the door behind her and locked it. I told her as she slowly approached, "I did a test run video. One second. Let me start again."

I stopped the recording and then started again, "Here we go. Fresh start. Now, Kim. Do you still want to be in my mini movie?"

"Of course."

"Sounds great. Then for the record, tell me your name and age."

Kim looked in the camera and stated, "Hi. I'm Kim Price. People say I look like that cheerleader character…"

I stopped her quick, "Hold it right there. For copyright reasons we can't say you look like her in the video. Today, you're just…Kim."

"Alright, my name is Kim Price. I'm twenty-one years old and I want to be in Frank's movie."

I turned the camera toward me and said, "If you think she looks younger than twenty-one, I do have the records and IDs of all my dancers on file. Kim is twenty-one."

Then I turned the camera back to Kim, "Do you agree on the payment we talked about?"

"Yes. Two hundred dollars for one starring role in your mini movie."

"And you'll do what I ask, since I'm the director?"

She shot me a very submissive look, "Yes, I'll do whatever you ask."

"Sounds great, I'll give you two more extra times on the main stage and a bonus for being an actress in my movie."

She walked slower to me, "Thanks baby. This will be so worth it."

Kim leaned down to kiss me, but I turned away, "Sorry, you know my number one rule. I don't kiss any of my girls on the lips."

"Why not? Is my lipstick smeared?"

I gave her two one hundred-dollar bills, "No kissing!" Then I smacked her ass.

Kim let out a little scream, "Oh, that stung."

"You want more?"

With an innocent look she confessed, "Maybe."

"Then get to work and be my actress in my video. Earn your money and be my slutty dancer."

Kim smiled, "Okay boss."

She walked away, very slowly and sexy, for just a second. She did this just so I could look at her ass.

I continued recording my video, "I love watching you do what you do. You have the best ass I've ever seen on a woman." Her cheeks made a lite bump from side to side as she walked. It tingled the senses in my eyeballs.

She bent over and grabbed her ankles as her rear end was staring at me. She smiled from under her legs, "I'm also very flexible too."

I ignored my camera for a moment, "That you are."

Kim walked back to me and looked deep into my eyes. She asked, "Ready?"

"Yep. And…action!"

First, she raised one leg and put it on my shoulder. My eyes could not get off what was right in from of them, "I see your still wet from the shower."

"Yep. The shower. That's it."

Kim smiled at me, put her leg down then hopped on my lap and gave me a lap dance.

I looked at her, "Have I told you that you're my favorite dancer."

"A few times."

Then I told the camera, "Kim has a hot body but at first, she wasn't into making any 'extra cash' isn't that, right?"

Kim moved her butt over my lap several times as she said, "Yep."

"But not anymore, right?"

She wrapped her arms around my neck and got so close I could smell her fresh breath, "What do you think?"

"I think you brushed your teeth before you came here."

She responded by opening her mouth and licking her top teeth.

I said in the video, "Kim swallowed her pride and is now my top money maker."

"Swallowed? Not yet."

"You are such a tease."

"That's what you pay me for."

Kim looked down, "I can see you're ready for what's next."

"Yes I am."

"Well then, time for me to do what you paid me for."

She got off my lap and lowered her body in front of me.

I pointed the camera at her. The action part of my mini movie was about to start.

Chapter 6

FRANK

As Kim took her money off my desk, she smiled and used her finger to wipe the extra spit from the corner of her mouth. With her other hand she looked at the two, hundred-dollar bills and said, "Easy money. Thanks again baby."

As she slowly walked out of my office I said to her, "No, thank you."

When she finally left my office, I took the SD card out of the camera and slid it in my laptop. As I slid my mouse past some pictures, I saw one of my dancers, Emma.

Emma, Trixie was her stage name, was an exceptionally good dancer. She knew what guys liked and she knew how to work the crowd.

Then my mind wondered and I started thinking about her tall sister Olivia. I hired her to be my bouncer a few weeks after her sister Emma came to work for me.

I shook my head in disbelief thinking about her, "Holy shit she's tall."

The smile on my face grew as I looked to the side and thought about Olivia for a moment. I wanted to have that freak of nature on my main stage so fucking bad. This girl would make me a killing. Guys love to get beat up and stepped on by someone five times bigger than them. Hell, I've seen a few guys do bad shit in here just so that Olivia can rough them up and kick them out.

I pulled up another picture of Olivia and smiled as I stroked my mustache. Olivia always did her job as a bouncer very well. Then I zoomed in closer on Olivia's big double 'D' boobs. They didn't look huge on her because of her massive height but I know women, those are double 'D's"

I sighed a distressing breath because I always tried to talk her into dancing, and she always refused.

One day, after talking to my sister Toni, she gave me an idea for a gimmick to get more people in the door. Female oil and mud wrestling. Toni is in the professional wrestling business. She told me that female wrestling is a huge enterprise now and I should get out of the slut bars.

She might be right but I was having too much fun.

I didn't want to give this up and move on to something else just yet. I just spent time with an amazing red head, Kim, who swallowed her pride and decided to advance her career in my club in a much faster way than just dancing. She's the smart one here.

I smirked a sarcastic smile as I looked at a few more pics of all the girls who currently worked for me. Kim, Becky, Coco, Emma, Mary Ann and a few part-timers too. I thought back to the day I had a bar meeting with everyone, except Olivia.

I told the girls in my club about my wrestling idea and that each girl who wrestled will get two hundred dollars for their 'performance' plus whatever tips they make.

All the girls agreed. Even the part-time dancers.

I knew that Olivia was never going to strip for me, so I saw wrestling as my chance to finally get her to work for me. The guys would bust a nut if they saw her beating up some poor girl in the mud. This was my one chance to have Olivia work for me and not as a bouncer.

Thinking back, I remember trying to convince her to wrestle was a challenge. A week before the wrestling was to start, in a private meeting with Olivia, I asked her if she would be interested in doing some wrestling matches. It didn't go well. "How would you like to be the star of my wrestling shows?"

Her droll face showed she didn't like that idea, "You're kidding, right?"

"My customers already know you as the tough bouncer. Guys would love to see you, the super tall girl, beating up on someone small."

She stared at me with contempt, "Rolling around in the mud in front of a bunch of people? No!"

"I bet you'll make a lot more than just a hundred and fifty dollars a night being my bouncer?"

"Probably, but my answer is still no. As your bouncer I'm respected. As a mud and oil wrestler, people will think I'm one of *your* girls, I'm not. The answer is, no."

Then she stormed out.

Convincing her to wrestle was not going to be easy but I was determined.

Looking up from my computer, I glanced at my door and realized I was completely distracted from what I was doing after Kim left.

"Oh yeah. Back to it." I said to myself.

I pulled the video off the SD card and moved the video of Kim into an invisible folder on my desktop. The folder wasn't labeled, nor could anyone see it unless you happen to scroll by it.

I deleted the test videos off my card, pulled it out of my computer and then put the SD card back in the camera. "There, all set for my next – actress."

Chapter 7

OLIVIA

When Frank first brought up the idea of me mud and oil wrestling, I thought he was joking. I laughed it off and told him flat-out, "No."

Frank wasn't the kind of guy to take no for an answer. He was persistent, like a mosquito buzzing in your ear at 3 a.m. A few days later, on a slow Wednesday night, he cornered me by the door. The bar was dead, just a handful of regulars nursing their drinks in the dim light. Frank leaned against the wall, his arms crossed, and gave me that sly grin of his.

"Slow night, isn't it?" he said, his voice dripping with false innocence.

I rolled my eyes. "It's the middle of the week, Frank. I don't expect a parade of horny men to magically show up on a Wednesday."

He shrugged, his grin widening. "Wrestling would bring people in. You know that."

I shot him a look. "Give it up, Frank. I'm not wrestling."

He stepped closer, his tone shifting to something almost convincing. "Olivia, listen. It's all just a performance. No one's going to get hurt. It's about putting on a show, that's all."

I crossed my arms, towering over him. "Fine. I'll referee but I'm not wrestling. End of discussion."

Frank held up his hands in mock surrender, but I could see the gears turning in his head. He wasn't done yet.

The night of the first mud wrestling match, the bar was packed. Frank had gotten word out about this female wrestling night. The promise of women rolling around in mud or oil was enough to draw a crowd. I stood by the pit, wearing the oversized black-and-white referee shirt Frank had special-ordered for me. The regular ones didn't come in my size, which was both a point of pride and a reminder of how out of place I felt in this whole circus.

The guys in the crowd were rowdy, hollering and whistling as the girls stepped into the pit. They squirmed and grappled; their movements more theatrical than athletic.

Every now and then, a top would come off, and the crowd would erupt in cheers. Some of the men even threw twenties into the pit, like they were dancing and this was a tip. I couldn't help but shake my head. Didn't they realize the money was just going to get ruined in the mud?

A few guys in the crowd shouted at me, "Hey, ref! When are you getting in the pit?"

I glared at them. "Never."

However, as I watched the match, I had to admit—Frank was right. It was all a performance. The girls weren't really fighting; they were putting on a show, playing up the drama for the crowd. It was sleazy, sure, but no one was getting hurt. Still, I wasn't about to join in. I wasn't one of

Frank's "girls." I was the bouncer, the one who kept the
peace. I had my dignity, and I wasn't going to trade it for a
few bucks.

That was until I didn't have a choice.

My truck was my lifeline. It got me to work, to the
store, to anywhere I needed to go. My sister and I worked at
the same bar, but we had different schedules, and I wasn't
about to rely on her for rides everywhere. So, when I hit a
deer on my way to work one night, it wasn't just the deer that
took the hit—it was my bank account, too.

The truck still ran, but the radiator was busted, and
the front end looked like it had gone ten rounds with a semi.
It wasn't safe to drive, and fixing it would cost more than I
had. I was stuck. I could either bum rides off my sister
indefinitely or find a way to make some extra cash—fast.

That's when Frank's offer started to look a little less
well, ridiculous.

I found him in his office, counting the night's take.
He looked up when I walked in, his eyebrows raised. "Olivia.
What can I do for you?"

I crossed my arms, leaning against the doorframe and
sighed. I could tell he knew what I was there for. He stopped
counting the money and asked me with a freakishly creepy
smile, "So, did you change your mind about wrestling?"

I wasn't about to let Frank know how desperate I was
for the money. He didn't need that kind of leverage over me.
So, when I walked into his office, I kept my cards close to my
chest. I sat down across from him, leaned forward, and

looked him straight in the eye. "Fine," I said. "I'll wrestle. On three conditions."

Frank's sleazy grin spread across his face like oil on water. "Lay 'em on me."

"One," I began, holding up a finger. "I wear a one-piece bathing suit. Always. I'm not one of your strippers, Frank. I'm not a slut like half the women here."

His grin faltered for a second, and he leaned back in his chair, feigning offense. "Not a slut like your sister, you mean?"

I shot up from my seat, looming over him like a storm cloud. "Hey, watch it. I know she's not old enough to work here, and I know you got her a fake ID."

He held up his hands, his voice dripping with mock innocence. "What? Me?"

"Yes, *you*," I snapped. "She's stubborn, and yeah, she's technically old enough to make her own decisions but she's not old enough to work here. Instead of letting her run off and get herself into trouble, I'm here to keep an eye on her. I know what she does in her free time, and I don't need your commentary on it."

Frank's eyes widened, and he leaned back even further, like he was trying to melt into his chair. "Okay, okay. Fair enough."

I sat back down, my tone icy. "Number two. I get that wrestling is a performance, so I'll make it look good. We'll put on a show, but that's it. I'm not stripping, and I'm not doing anything 'sexy.' Got it?"

He pouted like a child who'd been told he couldn't have dessert. "Really? Not even a few little booty shakes now and then?"

"No," I said, my voice sharp enough to cut glass.

He sighed, defeated. "Alright. What's number three?"

I leaned in close, my eyes locked on his. "I will never take my clothes off. Let me repeat that, Frank. You will *never* see me topless or naked in this bar. Got it?"

He nodded, a flicker of fear in his eyes. "Got it."

"And if any of the girls try to take my suit off while we're wrestling," I added, "I'll beat the living shit out of them, come for you next, and then quit."

Frank raised an eyebrow. "What about your sister?"

"Since she's underage," I said, my voice low and dangerous, "I'll make sure she leaves with me. I might even pay a visit to the cops to let them know about all the shady shit going on in this place. So don't piss me off, Frank."

He held up his hands again, his tone conciliatory. "Alright, alright. You've got yourself a deal."

"Good," I said, leaning back. "Now that we've settled that, when do you want me to start?"

"In a few weeks," he said, his grin returning. "I'll make sure our regulars know you'll be wrestling. They'll eat it up. I'll give you five hundred bucks a night since you'll be a 'special event' wrestler."

I raised an eyebrow. "More than the other girls, and I don't have to take my clothes off? Sweet deal."

"Yeah," he said, his grin turning sly. "Just keep your mouth shut about it."

I mimed zipping my lips shut.

"You'll always wrestle last," he added, tapping his desk excitedly. "You'll be the main attraction. Oh, and I've got this great idea—whoever wrestles you and loses—and let's be honest, they'll lose—has to do a 'walk of shame' to my office while you yell insults at them. You know, stuff like 'loser slut' and whatever. The crowd'll love it."

I stared at him, my expression flat. "No."

His grin faltered. "What? Why not? It'll be fun."

"It's degrading," I said. "I know most of these girls. I'm starting too actually like some of them. I'm not going to humiliate them in front of a crowd."

"It's just for show," he insisted.

"I don't care," I said, my voice firm. "I'm not doing it."

Frank leaned back, his grin turning sly again. "Olivia, have you ever watched WWE?"

"When I was a teenager, yeah. Not lately."

"It's the same thing," he said, waving a hand. "It's all an act. The girls here will be putting on a show. They'll insult each other, call each other bitches, shove faces in the mud—

none of it's real. The insults you'd yell? They'd know you don't mean it."

I narrowed my eyes. "Alright, once they're in your office, then what?"

"It's not like they're going to suck my dick or anything," he said, his voice pitching higher. "We'll let the crowd think what they want, but nothing's going to happen. It's all part of the show."

I still had my doubts, but I could see he wasn't going to drop it. "Fine," I said reluctantly. "I'll do the insults."

His grin widened, and he clapped his hands together. "Super. I can't wait to get this started."

As I left his office, I couldn't help but wonder what the hell I'd just agreed to. Looking back, I still don't know what I was thinking.

Chapter 8

OLIVIA

For the next two months, The Rat Hole hosted mud and oil wrestling once a week. My official job was still the bouncer, but I wrestled every other week. On my off weeks, I refed. The crowd couldn't get enough of the nights I stepped into the ring. When I wrestled, I went by the stage name *The Queen Bee.*

The first time I wrestled was in mud. My one-piece bathing suit was yellow and black, with horizontal stripes like a bee. I hated it. It clung awkwardly to my frame, and the colors made me feel like a walking caution sign. Once it was caked in mud, it didn't matter what it looked like.

I was nervous, though. More than I cared to admit. What would people think of me? Would they see me differently now that I wasn't just the bouncer? I stood backstage, my stomach churning, as the crowd's energy buzzed through the bar like an electric current. The air was thick with the smell of sweat, cheap beer, and the faint tang of the fake mud waiting in the pit.

Our DJ, doubled as the MC for the wrestling matches. His voice boomed over the speakers, "Are you guys having a good time tonight?"

The crowd erupted in cheers; their excitement palpable. I could feel it vibrating through the floor, up my legs, and into my chest. It was intoxicating and terrifying all at once.

"Sounds great!" Sam continued. "Again, my name's Sam Dancer, and I'm glad you're enjoying the show. Our final match tonight features two girls making their wrestling debut. First, give it up for Crystle Clear!"

The opening beats of *Pony* by Ginuwine blasted through the speakers as Crystle strutted out. She danced for the crowd, her movements practiced but lacking enthusiasm. I watched her closely, noticing the way her smile didn't quite reach her eyes. She didn't want to be here, but she didn't have a choice. I knew that feeling all too well.

When her entrance was over, Sam's voice rose again. "Ladies and gentlemen, wrestling for the first time ever, I give you... *The Queen Bee!*"

The opening bars of *Mama Said Knock You Out* by LL Cool J thundered through the bar. The curtain lifted, and I stepped out. For a split second, there was a collective gasp. Then the crowd exploded into cheers. The six-foot-six bouncer was finally wrestling, and they loved it.

I didn't strut or shake my ass like the other girls. I walked. Slowly. Deliberately. My face was serious, my eyes locked on the mud pit ahead. Intimidation was my strategy, and it was working. The song's aggressive beat matched my energy perfectly. This wasn't going to be a sexy dance—it was going to be a fight.

Crystle played her part well. She shook her head and yelled, "Oh hell no!" as if she hadn't known she'd be wrestling me. We'd talked backstage less than five minutes ago. She knew exactly what was coming.

She tried to turn and run, but the referee pushed her back into the ring. "Come on, don't be chicken," he said.

"She's going to kill me!" Crystle wailed, her voice dripping with mock despair. The crowd ate it up, laughing and cheering. I got it now—this was all part of the show. A performance. Entertainment.

We stepped into the pit, the cool mud squelching between my toes. It was thick and slippery, almost like wet clay, but cleaner than I'd expected. The fake mud was smooth, with a strange, almost oily texture that made it impossible to get a solid grip. It clung to my skin, cool and heavy, as we faced each other in the center of the pit.

I towered over Crystle, and the crowd loved the visual. I sloshed the mud around with my feet, kicking a little in her direction to play up the intimidation. She glared at me, her hands on her hips, and the crowd roared.

Then…we started. The moment we lunged at each other, the mud exploded around us, splattering the front row. The men closest to the pit laughed and cheered, wiping the mud from their faces like it was a badge of honor. The sound of our bodies hitting the mud was a wet, sloppy *thwack*, and within seconds, we were both caked in the stuff.

The mud was *slick*. Slicker than I'd imagined. Every movement was a struggle, my hands slipping off Crystle's arms, my feet sliding out from under me. My brain screamed, *It's so slippery!* but I kept my face stern, staying in character.

Surprisingly, I was having fun. The bar was packed, the crowd was roaring, and the adrenaline was pumping through me like a drug. Hearing them cheer my name—*Queen Bee! Queen Bee!*—was a thrill I hadn't expected.

The matches was a blur of mud, laughter, and exaggerated drama. I pinned Crystle three times in the first round and four times in the second. She hadn't pinned me once by the time we reached the third round. Money rained into the pit—mostly twenties, but I spotted a few fifties and even a couple of hundred-dollar bills. Before, I'd thought it was stupid. Now, knowing half of it would be mine, I didn't mind so much. Mud washes off. Money spends the same.

Sam's voice cut through the noise. "The score is seven to zero! Can Crystle get at least one pin before this is over? Let's find out. Ladies, begin!"

I went easy on her in the final round. She was exhausted, her movements sluggish. I lunged, knocking her onto her back, and pinned her again. She squirmed, but there was no way she was getting out from under me. When I let her up, she flicked mud off her hands and faced me again, her chest heaving.

I brushed my muddy hair out of my face and crawled toward her. We locked arms, and I used my weight to knock her down once more. This time, she landed on her stomach. I tried to grab her arm, but the mud made it impossible. She wriggled free, and I ended up sitting on her back, pulling her hair like the reins on a horse.

"Oh, fuck!" she screamed, her voice muffled by the mud. Her hair slipped from my grip, and I scooped up a handful of mud, smacking it against the side of her head. The crowd went wild.

I turned my head only for a second to see some of the men in the crowd were near salivating at the sight of us wrestling.

Crystal wiped the extra mud off her face, got back up on her knees and slid to me again. We skated toward each other quickly and smacked into each other like two charging rams. Our wet dirty bodies made a fantastic splattering noise. I managed to turn her body away from me so I curled my arms under her head and put her in a head lock. This didn't last long because she dropped her body and slid out of it.

Sam yelled, "Only a few seconds left, can Crystle get at least one pin from the giant Olivia?"

When I had Crystle flat on the mat, I leaned close to her ear and whispered, "Do you want me to let you have one?"

"That would be nice so I'm not a total loser."

On that note, she pushed me off her and threw mud at my face. As I was trying to wipe it away, she pounced on me and knocked me down. I could have effortlessly pushed her off, but I didn't. I let her have this one. She pulled my leg up and the crowd cheered for her. Nobody saw me but I smiled.

That one is all she's getting. I used my other leg and locked her head in a leg scissors. Keeping in mind this was all for show I yelled, "Fuck you, bitch. This was going to be a shut out until you did that."

She used her hands to try and move my legs away from her neck but my legs were like a vise grip. She struggled, she wiggled, but she couldn't get away. The squishing sound of mud between my legs and her neck sounded like the stirring of mac-and-cheese.

The ref had to tap my shoulder to make me let her go. As our dirty rumble was about to end, I jumped on her, pulled her legs up toward her neck and pinned her again. She wiggled and squirmed in the murky brown stuff, but she wasn't going anywhere. Her body was worn-out from three rounds of wrestling. I could tell she was done.

While I pushed Crystle's leg up for a pin, my long wet dirty hair covered her face as I told her, "This was fun. Sorry you lost."

"It's okay. I expected it. My whole-body hurts."

"You do know what comes next, right?"

"Humiliation?"

"Yep, Frank's idea."

"As if losing to you wasn't bad enough. Whatever. Let's get this over with."

DING! When the final bell rang, Sam announced my victory. "With a score of nine to one, your winner this evening is *The Queen Bee!*"

The crowd erupted. I stood in the pit, my chest heaving, mud dripping from my hair and body. Sam raised my hand in victory, as I put my foot on Crystle's body in the mud put.

Everyone stood up as those words brought a roaring cheer to the crowd and a scowl to Crystel's face. For the moment, I was drunk from the attention. I did what Frank asked and shouted degrading comments to her, "Ha bitch! You lost! Do the walk of shame, you loser slut."

I yelled more demeaning comments as Crystal walked to Frank's office with her head hanging low still covered in mud.

Sam raised my hand up for a victory again as the door to Frank's office slammed shut. It was well known that I was not a dancer nor did I date a lot like most of the girls here.

A few weeks ago, I didn't want to have anything to do with yelling at my friends. Turns out, I enjoyed yelling the humiliating comments.

It was fun to let out some anger, even though it wasn't really real, "That's one loser slut who lost to me, who will be next?"

I pointed to another dancer named, Becky, "Will it be you?" Then I pointed to my sister, "Or you!"

Later, as we were about to close up for the night, we were all walking to our cars. I asked Crystle, "You know what I said after we wrestled, it was just for show. You know that, right?"

She laughed, "Duh!"

"I have to know, what happened in Frank's office?"

She never looked at me as she answered, "Nothing."

"Nothing? Great, that was just for show then too. I thought for sure he would take advantage of some of the girls. So far it looks like when I wrestle it brings him lots of business and more money. He knows better than to fuck it up."

She answered in a very mellow voice, "Yep."

"Okay, maybe I'll wrestle you again sometime."

She did her best to crack a smile, "No. This will be my last night. I earned all the money I needed so I'm moving on to bigger and better things."

I was a little disappointed, "But you just started."

"Yeah, well — it was fun, but this life isn't for me."

I feared the worst, "Oh my Gosh, I didn't hurt you, did I?"

"No. I'll be fine. I was talking about stripping, not the wrestling."

As Emma approached her car, I told Crystle, "Alright then, keep in touch."

Crystle didn't answer. She got in her car and drove off.

Emma was excited to know how much I made tonight, "So, how did you do?"

"First off, I'm driving. I see you're a little tipsy."

She threw her keys to me, "Fine, whatever. Here."

When we got in her car, Emma's leg bounced up and down like Thumper in Bambi as she asked again, "Come on, I'm dying to know."

"With my base pay from Frank and tips, I made just over two thousand dollars in one flippin night."

Emma's jaw hit the floorboard, "Are you fucking kidding me? You didn't even do anything!"

I laughed a little. She was so jealous I made a killing, and I never took my clothes off, "Yes, I did. I wrestled."

"You know what I mean? You didn't have to get naked."

As I started the car I told her, "I'm sure I only made that much because it's my first time. People have been dying to see me wrestle."

"Yes, they have."

"Actually, I could have made a thousand dollars more, but I turned it down."

"What the fuck? How?"

While I pulled out of the parking lot I said, "Some young techie genius wanted me to give him a private show in one of Frank's special private booths, while I was still covered in mud."

"Those are fun. Sounds…dirty."

I shook my head from the terrible joke, "That was bad and…what? Ewww! No. He wanted me to yell at him and watch him crank one out from the other side of a window. No thanks."

"Well, you are a big, tall girl. You could make a killing as a dominatrix. I'm just sayin'"

I didn't want to hear that, "Please stop talking."

The second time I wrestled, it was in baby oil. It wasn't as messy as mud, but it was far more slippery. The air smelled faintly of coconut and aloe, a stark contrast to the usual stench of sweat and stale beer that clung to The Rat Hole. The oil glistened under the bar's dim lights, catching every movement like liquid gold. It was almost beautiful, in a cheap, tawdry way.

This time, I wrestled my sister—Emma, or Trixie, as she called herself here. It was her first time wrestling, and she played her part perfectly. She strutted out to the crowd, her movements exaggerated and playful, her smile wide and fake. She was the embodiment of the "slutty dancer" persona, and the crowd loved her for it.

From the roar that erupted when my name was announced, it was clear they'd come to see me. They wanted the six-foot-six bouncer, the giantess, to dominate someone again.

I stepped into the oil-slick ring, my one-piece bathing suit clinging to me like a second skin. The oil was cool at first, sending a shiver up my legs as I waded in but it quickly warmed against my skin, slick and heavy, making every movement feel deliberate and precarious.

Emma and I faced each other, the crowd's energy buzzing around us like a swarm of bees. She smirked at me, her eyes glinting with mischief, and I knew she was going to make this as dramatic as possible.

We made it look good. She played the fun, flirty dancer, while I was the stoic, no-nonsense bouncer. The crowd ate it up. Most of the time, she stayed in character, but every now and then, she'd slip—literally and figuratively. She'd laugh, her giggles breaking through her performance as she struggled to keep her footing. "It's so slippery!" she exclaimed at one point, her voice high and breathless.

I thought the same thing, but I didn't let it show. I stayed in character, my face stern, my movements deliberate. I was here to win, not to play.

As the match went on, I couldn't help but notice the way the crowd watched us. Their eyes were hungry, their cheers raucous and lewd. It was different from when I was the bouncer. Back then, they feared me. Respected me. Now, they were just… watching.

I pinned Emma three times in quick succession, her body sliding against mine in the oil, her laughter turning to exaggerated groans of defeat.

When the final bell rang, I stood over her, my chest heaving, the oil glistening on my skin. Sam announced my victory, and the crowd erupted. I pointed at Emma, my voice booming, "Ha, bitch! I won. It's 'walk of shame' time. See Frank, you loser slut."

Emma played her part perfectly, her head lowered as she walked across the stage topless, the crowd laughing and jeering. I raised my arms in victory, my voice dripping with mock arrogance. "Who dares to challenge me next?"

I pointed to Becky, then to Coco, my tone taunting. "Will it be you? Or you? Maybe next time, you'll lose to me and have to do the slut walk of shame."

The crowd roared, their laughter and cheers feeding into my performance.

However, as I stood there, my arms raised, the oil cooling on my skin, I felt a shift. My eyes scanned the room, taking in the sea of faces—mostly men, their eyes glued to me. One guy in particular caught my attention. He was grabbing his crotch, adjusting himself, his gaze fixed on me with a hunger that made my stomach turn.

I felt exposed in a way I never had before. As a bouncer, I was in control. People feared me. Respected me. But here, in the ring, I was just part of the show. A spectacle. The realization hit me like a punch to the gut, and for a moment, I felt small. Vulnerable.

I quickly pushed the feeling aside, bending down to scoop up the loose bills scattered across the oily mat. Twenties, fifties, even a few hundred-dollar bills—twelve hundred dollars in total. It was a lot of money for just a few minutes of wrestling. As I walked backstage, the oil still clinging to my skin, I couldn't shake the unease that had settled over me.

This wasn't me. This wasn't who I was supposed to be. However, the sound of the crowd's cheers echoed in my ears, I couldn't deny the thrill that came with it. The power. The attention. That scared me more than anything.

A few weeks later, during another mud wrestling night, I noticed something that made my skin crawl. The way the men watched me had changed. It wasn't about the match anymore—it wasn't about winning or losing. Their eyes were glued to me, not with admiration or excitement, but with a creeping, leering hunger. They didn't care about the fight. They just wanted to see if my top would come off, if the mud would slide away and reveal something they had no right to see.

I won, of course. I always won. As I walked backstage, my body caked in thick, drying mud, I felt hollow. A few strands of wet, dirty hair kept falling into my face, no matter how many times I pushed them back. They clung to my cheeks, sticky and stubborn, like the shame I couldn't shake.

My hair wasn't the only thing bothering me. My chest felt heavy, like a weight was pressing down on me, and I struggled to swallow the lump in my throat. I looked down at myself, at the thick brown sludge covering my skin, and felt a wave of disgust. This wasn't me. This wasn't who I was supposed to be.

I stood by the bathroom door, waiting for my turn in the shower, when Kim and Coco walked out, both naked and still dripping wet. Kim smirked at me, her perfect body glistening under the fluorescent lights. "Saving water?" I asked, my voice dripping with sarcasm.

Coco giggled, her laughter light and carefree. "Yep."

As Coco walked away, Kim lingered, her eyes scanning my mud-streaked body. "Did you win again?" she asked, her tone almost teasing.

"What do you think?" I snapped, my patience wearing thin.

Kim shrugged, oblivious to the storm raging inside me. "You know, this slick wrestling is fun, but I hate the mud. Everything gets so dirty. I like oil better."

I wasn't in the mood for small talk. "Listen, Kim," I said, my voice sharp. "I don't mean to be a bitch, but I just want to get this shit off me."

She rolled her eyes and walked past me, her naked body a stark reminder of everything I wasn't. I closed the bathroom door behind me and stepped into the shower, the sound of the water hitting the tiles echoing in the small space.

I pressed my hand against the wall, letting the water run over my head. It was warm, almost too warm, but I didn't care. I needed it to wash away the dirt, the grime, the feeling of being watched like a piece of meat.

No matter how hard I scrubbed, I couldn't shake the heaviness in my chest.

As the water cascaded over me, my mind raced. Kim with her perfect body, my sister with her flirtatious confidence, Coco with her flawless skin—they all seemed to fit in here. They thrived in this world of cheap thrills and fake smiles. But me? I was the giant. The bouncer. The one who was supposed to command respect, not strip it away layer by layer.

I peeled back the shower curtain, glancing behind me to make sure I was alone. The room was empty.

The weight of everything I was feeling pressed down on me until I couldn't hold it back anymore. I cried. Quietly, so no one would hear, but the tears came anyway, mixing with the water running down my face.

This wrestling crap was draining me. Every match chipped away at the pride and respect I'd worked so hard to build. The water washed away the mud, but it couldn't wash away the shame, the anger, the hurt. I felt exposed in a way I never had before, like I was becoming one of the girls I'd always looked down on. I wasn't like them. I wasn't a slut. I wasn't here to be ogled or objectified. The way those men looked at me—like I was nothing more than a fantasy—made me feel like I was losing myself.

I didn't want to do this anymore.

But I didn't quit. I couldn't. In a few short weeks, I'd have enough money saved for a new car, and then I'd be done. I'd walk away from this and never look back. Until then, I had to keep going. I had to swallow my pride, no matter how much it hurt.

I let the water cover my face, washing away the last of my tears. I looked down and saw that most of the mud was gone, but the ache in my chest remained. I reached for the shampoo, my hands trembling slightly, and lathered up, scrubbing until my skin felt raw.

I would get through this. I had to. As I stood there, the water running over me, I couldn't help but wonder how much of myself I'd have left by the time it was over.

Chapter 9

FRANK

Secretly I was hoping that Olivia's bathing suit would slip off in all the mud and oil, but it never did.

My patience was wearing thin waiting to see Olivia's big tits. I came up with an idea to get her naked or at least topless. This idea would put all the blame on the dancer who did this for me and none of the blame on me.

One of my dancers, Becky Powers, came into my office before we closed up for the night, "You wanted to see me."

"Becky, I did a little digging. Are you Italian?"

"Half. My dad's last name is Regatta and my mom's maiden name is Powers. They're divorced now but I use her maiden name. I liked Powers better. Becky Powers is a better show name."

"I do like that show name but never forget where you came from, I'm Italian too."

She said sarcastically, "No kidding."

"Did my gold chains give it away?"

"That and the hair."

"Anyway, how would you like to make an extra five hundred bucks?"

"Are you offering more for your little bonus? I'm really tired right now but what the hell, five hundred bucks is..."

I giggled and stopped her, "No, it's not that."

"Oh?"

"Olivia has wrestled three times now."

"Yeah."

I cocked my head to the side and asked, "Don't you find it strange that she's been rolling around in the mud and oil for a few weeks and her top has never come off yet?"

"Not really. She told us before we started this wrestling thing that if anyone of us tried that she'd beat the shit out of us. She scares me."

I tilted in toward her raising my eye brows, "How scared?"

"I've seen her throw out grown men. Scared enough."

I smiled a very mischievous grin and laid five one-hundred-dollar bills in front of her. "Will this give you courage?"

She finally got where I was going, "Oh, OH, you want to pay me to try and rip her top off."

I pointed my finger at her and winked, "Now you're catching on."

"Tempting but it will take more than just five hundred dollars to - pull off - the impossible."

Then I laid another five hundred dollars down in front of her on my desk.

She saw all the money. It was like the bait on a fishing line. I could tell she was thinking about it, "You know, she's the only one that has never shown any skin."

I added, "She's also the only one of all my full-time employees that has never taken me up on the 'bonus' offer either."

"Seriously?"

"Yep. Well, her and that Crystle girl but she didn't last long so I don't count her."

"Seriously, it's the easiest two hundred bucks I ever made. I'll see what I can do to change her mind for you."

I stopped her from getting to far ahead, "Let's start with her boobs first."

She smiled as she said, "A thousand bucks to try and rip Olivia's top off?"

I held more cash in my hand and added, "If her top does come off, I'll give you five hundred more."

Her jaw almost hit the floor as she tried to say, "Fifteen hundred dollars?"

She finally took the bait, "Alright, I'll do it. Our wrestling matches are for show. What's the worst that could happen?"

In my mind I thought, 'What's the worst that could happen? She's going to turn your face into ground beef, that's what's going to happen.'

Out loud I told her, "Good. This weekend is Olivia's turn to ref so let's plant the seeds of aggression this weekend when you wrestle her sister."

We both smiled at each other like an evil plot was brewing. The only thing that was missing was a maniacal laugh.

That weekend, when Becky mud wrestled Emma, Olivia called a pin for her sister, but Becky got pissed. "What do you mean she pinned me? There's no way that was a pin!"

I watched as Becky started arguing with this giant ass woman. It didn't matter if she had a pin or not, the point was to start some shit.

The crowd ate it up and thought it was part of the show. My plan was slowly taking shape.

A couple of weeks later, at the next wrestling event, to make sure Olivia's sister didn't catch on to what I was doing, I gave Emma the rest of the night off, with pay. Luckly, Olivia didn't think anything was up when I gave her sister the night off.

To press Olivia's buttons, I changed things up a bit too. It was an oil wrestling night, so I went into the girls dressing room to tell them the news about my change, "Listen girls, tonight we're going to use cooking oil instead of baby oil."

Becky didn't care but a few of the girls did. Olivia hated it the most, "What the hell, Frank? That shit stinks and it will take forever to clean out of my hair."

"Cooking oil is a lot cheaper than baby oil. A gallon of cooking oil costs ten dollars. A gallon of baby oil costs five times as much."

Truthfully, the cost didn't matter to me at all. Hell, I'm making money hand over foot in this place. The cooking oil was another ingredient that I needed to start a fight before the wrestling match. This way Becky would have an excuse to be mad at Olivia and take off her top.

First, Olivia was mad at me for changing the type of oil and then Becky called Olivia a whiny bitch for complaining about it.

It's as if I was making a Spicy Italian Soup. I just added the vegetable oil. Next comes the spicy Italian sausage and onions and then stir. I can't wait to see my little spicy Italian peal the layers off that onion.

This was the spat just before the match that I was waiting for. A real fight was starting to brew. I could feel it in the air!

Tonight, will be the night I will finally see Olivia topless.

Chapter 10

JAXON

The night of my bachelor party arrived, and it was one of those rare, perfect summer evenings. The sky was a deep, clear indigo, dotted with stars, and the air was warm but not stifling, carrying the faint scent of rain on the horizon. It was the kind of night that made you want to stay outside, but here I was, heading into *The Rat Hole*, a gentleman's club with a name that sounded more like a dive bar than a strip club.

My friends had insisted it would be fun, but I wasn't so sure. Strippers, topless dancers, and lap dances weren't exactly my idea of a good time. Still, my fiancée had encouraged me to go, and I didn't want to disappoint my friends, so I played along.

As we pulled up to the place, I couldn't help but laugh. The building looked like an old barn, its weathered wood and rusted metal siding giving it a distinctly rural vibe. "Are we in the right place?" I asked, half-joking.

Jerry Stanford, the one guy I'd hoped wouldn't show up, slapped me hard on the back and barked, "I've been here a few times. The barn's a decoy. You'll see."

Jerry was thirty-five, with a horseshoe of thinning hair and a thick mustache that made him look like he'd wandered off the set of a '70s rock documentary. He was a backstabbing asshole at work, the kind of guy who'd steal clients and then act like it was no big deal. I couldn't stand him, but here he was, grinning like he'd just won the lottery.

We parked in what felt like the middle of nowhere, walked up to a concrete pillar, and opened a door that led to a staircase. The steps were lit like an airport runway, glowing strips of light guiding us downward. The air grew cooler as we descended, and the faint hum of bass from the club below vibrated through the walls. By the time we reached the bottom, my phone had no signal, which made me uneasy. Being cut off from the outside world felt like a bad omen.

At the entrance, I caught a glimpse of the bouncer—a towering figure with long, wavy brown hair and a "Security" label on their shirt. I couldn't tell if they were a man or a woman, but before I could get a better look, they disappeared into the club.

Inside, the place was a sensory overload. The air was thick with the mingling scents of cheap perfume, sweat, and the faint tang of alcohol. A redhead with curves that defied gravity was dancing on a pole on a small stage, her movements hypnotic.

What really caught my eye was the massive square pool on the main stage, surrounded by gallon jugs of vegetable oil. The place was surprisingly upscale for a strip club, with plush seating, sleek bars, and mood lighting that gave it a nightclub vibe. Most of the women wore bikinis or lingerie, though a few strutted around topless, their confidence both impressive and unsettling.

Evan Downs, the new guy at work, patted me on the back. At twenty-eight, he was two years younger than me, but his baby face and spiky hair made him look even younger. "Rick told me all about tonight," he said, grinning. "You're going to love it."

Rick Lopez, the oldest in our group and the only one wearing a suit, chuckled. "Hey, no spoilers!" Rick was in his forties, with a sharp jawline and a confidence that came from being the wealthiest guy in the room. His suit probably cost more than my car.

I laughed, gesturing to the pool and the oil jugs. "No spoilers? Really? It's pretty obvious what the entertainment is."

Rick's smile widened. "Ah, but you don't know the best part."

We found a table after Jerry, true to form, rudely asked a dancer named Coco to clear one for us. "Hey, be nice," I said, shooting him a look. "She's not the busboy."

Jerry smirked. "Of course, she's not. Look at the size of her tits."

I leaned over to Rick. "Who invited him again?"

"He got here on a technicality. You invited Evan, and he brought Jerry as his plus one."

"Oh, right," I muttered, regretting my generosity.

The night's entertainment was female oil wrestling, which my friends thought would be right up my alley since I'm a wrestling promoter. They weren't wrong—men's oil wrestling is the national sport in Turkey, and while I don't follow it, I'd much rather watch women in bikinis wrestle than large, hairy men. Still, the whole thing felt… off.

We settled at the table, five of us with a clear view of the stage. Jerry, however, sat as far back as possible. Evan raised an eyebrow. "Is there a reason you're hiding back there?"

"You guys are sitting in the splash zone."

"And that's a problem, why?"

"I'm allergic to that oil asshole," Jerry said, his tone defensive. "I break out in a rash if it touches my skin. I only use organic extra virgin olive oil at home. They're using the cheap shit."

Our waitress, Mary Ann, arrived to take our orders. She was stunning—a blonde with piercing blue eyes, wearing a cowboy hat and a white bikini with fringe that swayed as she moved. "Hey y'all," she drawled. "I'm Mary Ann. I'll be gettin' your drinks tonight."

Rick, ever the showman, announced, "We're here to celebrate Jaxon's last night as a single man."

"Last night?" I corrected. "I'm not getting married for a few weeks."

Rick waved me off. "Doesn't matter. This is your night to let loose. Have fun!"

I ordered a soda, which earned me a chorus of groans from the group. "Come on, dude," Jerry said, slamming his hand on the table. "It took us forever to drag you here. The least you can do is get drunk with us."

Mary Ann smirked. "He's got a point, sugar. It's your special night. Have a little fun."

"I'll stick with sugary drinks," I said firmly. "Keep them dry."

She shrugged. "Suit yourself, sugar."

Rick smiled at her and said, "I'll have a glass of wine."

Jerry shouted, "Pussy! Give me a beer and a shot of tequila."

Rick got Mary Ann's attention, "Hey, is The Queen Bee wrestling tonight?"

"She sure is honey."

Rick leaned in and whispered something to her, slipping her a wad of cash. I caught a glimpse of hundred-dollar bills and frowned. "Dude, what are you doing?"

Mary Ann's eyes widened as she counted the money. "For this amount, sugar, I'll make sure she'll suck his cock too."

I nearly choked. "No, no. That won't be necessary."

She laughed, her voice light and teasing. "Relax, sugar. I was kidding. We're entertainers, not prostitutes."

Jerry, of course, couldn't resist. "Entertainers, huh? How much *would* that cost?"

I shot him a glare. "Ignore him. He's an idiot."

Mary Ann leaned down to me; her breath warm against my ear. "Sugar, I've worked here for over a year. I deal with guys like him all the time."

She straightened up and flashed us a smile. "Be back lickity-split, boys."

As she walked away, I glanced back at the stage, my eyes lingering on the pool and the jugs of oil. I couldn't help but wonder: who was this Queen Bee, and was she really worth the money Rick had just thrown around?

Chapter 11

JAXON

A half hour had passed, and the air in The Rat Hole was electric with anticipation. The dim lighting cast a warm, amber glow over the room, and the low hum of chatter and laughter buzzed like a live wire. The scent of stale beer, cheap perfume, and the dull funky smell of frying oil hung in the air, mingling with the faint metallic undertone of the club's underground location. The stage was set, the pool-like ring glistening under the spotlight, waiting to be transformed into a slippery battleground.

The DJ, stepped up to the mic, his voice booming through the speakers. "Good evening, everyone! My name is Sam Dancer, and I'll be your ringside announcer tonight. You're in for a treat because, in our main event, *The Queen Bee* will be wrestling for you!"

The room erupted in cheers, the sound swelling like a wave. The crowd's energy was palpable, a mix of excitement and raw, unfiltered enthusiasm. It was clear that The Queen Bee was a fan favorite, someone they'd never seen before but I couldn't wait to see if the audience was this excited for her. Whistles, shouts, and clapping filled the air, and the floor seemed to vibrate with the collective energy of the room.

Sam grinned, feeding off the crowd's reaction. "Tonight is oil wrestling night! Now, Frank, the owner of this fine establishment"—he paused for effect, his tone dripping with mock seriousness—"is a bit of a tightwad when it comes to money. He wanted us to use old fry oil from the kitchen."

The crowd burst into laughter, the sound echoing off the walls. Sam waited for it to die down before continuing.

"I'm kidding, folks. We're changing things up a bit tonight. Instead of baby oil, we'll be using cooking oil. Let's get this place nice and slippery!"

The audience roared, their cheers rising to a deafening crescendo as two dancers stepped forward, each holding a gallon jug of vegetable oil. They unscrewed the caps and began pouring the oil into the ring, the golden liquid glinting under the lights as it pooled and spread. The smell of the oil was faint but distinct, adding another layer to the sensory overload of the room.

Sam watched as the dancers worked, his voice carrying over the noise. "While my friends here oil up the ring, let me tell you what you're in for tonight. We've got five matches lined up for your entertainment, and our fifth match is the main event. Trust me, you won't want to miss it."

When the dancers finished, they waved to the crowd, their movements exaggerated and playful. Sam gestured to them. "Thank you, ladies. Now, let me introduce Amber, our ring girl for the evening." A blonde in a sequined bikini stepped forward, holding a round card. "She'll be keeping track of the rounds for us. And on my right, we have the lovely Kitty."

Kitty, a brunette with a sly smile, stood next to Sam. At his cue, she shrugged off her robe to reveal a black-and-white striped referee shirt. The crowd whistled and cheered as she struck a pose, her confidence radiating. "Kitty will be our referee tonight," Sam announced.

"Now, these two won't be fighting, but I assure you, we've got ten girls who are ready to get greased up for your fighting pleasure. Are you ready?"

The crowd's response was thunderous. "Yeah!" some shouted, while others bellowed, "HELL YEAH!" The energy in the room was infectious, a mix of anticipation and raw, unfiltered excitement.

The first three matches flew by, each one a spectacle of exaggerated moves, playful banter, and the occasional wardrobe malfunction. The women put on a show, shaking their hips, squeezing their chests, and playing up the drama for the crowd. Tops came off, oil splashed everywhere, and the audience ate it up, their cheers and laughter filling the room.

As the matches dragged on, I found myself growing bored. The novelty of oil wrestling had worn off, and the repetitive nature of the performances left me glancing at the clock. The crowd, however, remained fully engaged, their enthusiasm never waning. They cheered, jeered, and threw money into the ring, their energy feeding into the spectacle.

I couldn't wait for the main event. Main events were always something special, and I had a feeling The Queen Bee would deliver.

For now, I was stuck in the lull, counting down the minutes until the real show began.

When the fourth match started, I walked to the bathroom to pee but I also texted Noa. There was very little reception down here so I was amazed my text went through. It did, but very slowly.

The guys took me to see female oil wrestling.

Sounds fun.

Not really. It's generally a sexy oil show.

Oh.

More touchy feely then actual wrestling or fighting.

Are you having fun?

Not really.

I'll come home as soon as we're done here.

K.

The fourth match was winding down, the third round dragging on as Coco and Kim grappled in the oil-slick ring. Coco, her dark skin glistening under the lights, yanked on Kim's leg, sending the redhead tumbling backward with a wet *splat*. The oil rippled around her, droplets flying into the air like golden rain. I glanced at Jerry, who flinched as if he'd been hit, even though the oil didn't come anywhere near him. His over-the-top reaction almost made me laugh, but the spectacle in front of me was too absurd to find amusing.

Kim landed on her back, her chest heaving as Coco straddled her, Coco's legs locking around Kim's torso.

The crowd roared, their cheers rising to a fever pitch as Coco leaned forward, her hands gripping Kim's breasts and squeezing them together. Kim played along, arching her back and letting out an exaggerated moan that sent the audience into a frenzy. The oil made their bodies gleam, every movement slick and exaggerated, their curves highlighted by the golden sheen.

I sighed, leaning back in my chair. This wasn't wrestling. This was… something else entirely. A performance, sure, but one that felt more like a parody of the sport I loved.

The crowd didn't seem to care—they were eating it up, their eyes glued to the stage, their voices hoarse from shouting.

My friends were no different. Rick was grinning like a kid in a candy store, Evan was leaning forward so far, I thought he might fall out of his chair, and even Jerry, for all his bluster, was staring intently, his mustache twitching as he muttered something under his breath.

I glanced around the room, taking in the scene. The air was thick with the smell of oil and sweat, the faint hint of alcohol lingering beneath it. The lights reflected off the slick surfaces, casting the room in a warm, golden glow. The women on stage were undeniably stunning, their bodies glistening and their movements fluid,

For me, the whole thing felt… hollow. It was all for show, all for the crowd's pleasure, and I couldn't help but feel disconnected from it. I texted Noa again.

I really want to come home now. This is dull.

I'm sorry.

Stay. Have fun. Maybe the best part is yet to come.

You're probably right.

The last match is about to start.

The fourth match ended with a splash—literally. Kim, the redhead with the big boobs, had "won" after Coco pinned her in a move that involved more chest-squeezing than actual wrestling.

The crowd erupted in cheers as Kim shook her oil-slicked chest for the audience, her laughter echoing through the room. Sam, the ever-charismatic MC, stepped up to the mic. "And the winner between Kim and Coco is… Kim!"

The applause was deafening, but Coco wasn't having it. She playfully shoved Kim out of the way, her dark skin glistening under the lights as she mock-glared at the crowd.

"Oh no," Sam said, his voice dripping with faux concern. "Looks like Coco isn't too happy with that decision."

Kim grabbed a towel, wrapped it around her chest, and strutted offstage, her hips swaying as the crowd whistled and cheered. The energy in the room was electric, a mix of laughter, shouts, and the occasional drunken slur.

The real show was just about to begin.

Sam's voice boomed through the speakers, cutting through the noise. "Alright, ladies and gentlemen! We've reached the best part of the evening. It's time for the main event!"

The crowd erupted, their chants rising like a tidal wave. "Queen Bee! Queen Bee! Queen Bee!"

Sam held up a hand, trying to quiet them down. "Alright, alright. Settle down now. We'll get to the last match in a second." The room grew quieter, but the anticipation was palpable, like a coiled spring ready to snap. "Before we get to our final wrestling match of the evening, I need to call someone to the stage. Tonight is a special night. It's the bachelor party for Jaxon Anderson!"

My stomach dropped. All eyes turned to me as Sam continued, "Jaxon's getting married in a few weeks, so his friends wanted to give him something he'll never forget. The chance to oil up The Queen Bee and watch the match from the sidelines. Come on up here, Jaxon!"

The crowd roared, their cheers and whistles echoing in my ears as I stood up. My friends clapped and hollered, their grins wide and knowing. I shot Rick a look, but he just shrugged, his smirk telling me he'd planned this all along. I climbed onto the stage, the lights blinding me for a moment as I adjusted to the sudden spotlight.

Sam handed me a forty-ounce bottle of cooking oil. "Here," he said, his tone playful. "Hold onto this like you're about to cook up something special."

I gripped the bottle, feeling the cool plastic against my palm. Sam leaned in, his voice carrying over the mic. "Have you been here before?"

"No," I said, shaking my head. "Never."

"Oh, then you don't know anything about The Queen Bee, do you?"

"Nope."

Sam's grin widened as he brought over a gallon jug of oil and slammed it down next to me. "I don't think the little bottle will be enough. You might need this."

The crowd erupted in laughter, their voices a cacophony of amusement. I forced a smile, playing along even though I felt like a fish out of water.

Sam chuckled, patting me on the back. "I'm kidding. But seriously, you've never been here or heard of The Queen Bee?"

"Nope," I said again, my voice steady despite the nerves creeping in.

"Boy, are you in for a surprise," Sam said, his tone teasing. He walked away, adding, "Don't forget, you can take as many pictures of the girls wrestling as you'd like. It's your bachelor party, and you've got a front-row seat."

"Alright," I said, though I had no intention of taking pictures. The crowd's energy was overwhelming, their cheers and shouts filling the room like a living thing. Sam turned back to the audience, his voice rising. "Everybody, are you ready for tonight's main event?"

The response was deafening. The crowd roared, their excitement vibrating through the floor and up into my chest. It was like standing in the middle of a thunderstorm, the energy raw and electric.

Sam's voice cut through the noise. "Finally, the match you've all been waiting for. The battle between The Queen Bee and Becky 'The Bomb' Powers!"

The crowd went wild, their cheers rising to a fever pitch. Sam continued, "First, let me introduce to you Becky. She stands five feet nine inches tall and weighs in at one hundred and fifty-eight pounds. It's Becky 'The Bomb' Powers!"

The opening notes of *You Dropped a Bomb on Me* by The Gap Band blasted through the speakers, the bass reverberating in my chest. Becky strutted out, her confidence radiating as she danced to the beat. She wore a black leather jacket and nothing else, her long legs drawing every eye in the room.

As she reached the edge of the stage, she shrugged off the jacket, revealing a red and black bikini that left little to the imagination. She tossed the jacket to Evan, who caught it with a grin.

Jerry leaned over, his voice loud and obnoxious. "Dude, you're so lucky. You got a souvenir!"

I rolled my eyes. "It's her leather jacket. I'm sure he has to give it back."

"Fuck no, man. Keep it," Jerry said, his tone dripping with envy. I shook my head, tuning him out as Becky continued her performance.

She sauntered over to a Latino man in the front row, pulling him up to the stage. "What's your name?" Sam asked, holding the mic out to him.

"Carlo," the man said, his voice barely audible over the music.

Becky sat on his lap, facing him, and shook her head to the beat. "Oh, Carlo," she purred, her voice sultry. "Is that a phone in your pocket, or are you just happy to see me?"

The crowd erupted in laughter, their cheers and whistles filling the room. Becky's performance was over-the-top, her every move designed to entertain. When the song ended, she turned to face the wrestling pit, her smile wide and playful.

Sam stepped back up to the mic, his voice rising. "Now, it's time for me to introduce Becky's challenger. You regulars know her because she's hard to miss. She stands six feet six inches tall and weighs in at two hundred and two pounds. She's the one none of you should ever want to mess with. It's… *The Queen Bee!*"

The opening notes of *The Rocky Theme* blared through the speakers, the iconic trumpets sending a jolt of energy through the room. When The Rocky theme started blaring through the speakers, I knew right away this person was something different. Rocky is a fighter, not a dancer.

The crowd jumped to their feet, their cheers deafening as The Queen Bee emerged from backstage. My jaw dropped. She was enormous—tall, muscular, and radiating an intensity that made everyone else in the room seem small.

Wait… was that the security guard I'd seen earlier?

The Queen Bee didn't strut or dance. She walked, her movements deliberate and powerful, like a predator stalking its prey. She wore a robe, the kind boxers wear before a fight, but I could see the black and yellow stripes of her one-piece bathing suit underneath. The crowd's excitement was ecstatic, their cheers and shouts rising to a crescendo as she approached the ring.

When she reached my corner, I managed a weak, "Hi."

She didn't smile. She just nodded, her expression serious as she shrugged off her robe and handed it to me.

"Hi," she said, her voice low and no-nonsense. Nothing else. No playful banter, no flirtatious smile. Just… intensity.

Becky, meanwhile, was lying on the edge of the ring, letting Carlo pour oil over her. She squeezed her chest and put on a show, her laughter echoing through the room. The Queen Bee, on the other hand, stood still, her arms crossed as she waited for me to start.

"Where do you want me to start?" I asked, holding up the bottle of oil.

"It doesn't matter," she said, her tone blunt. "This shit stinks, and it's going to be a mess. Just start pouring."

I hesitated, then began pouring the oil over her shoulders and back. She didn't move, didn't react, her expression stoic. "Is something wrong?" I asked, trying to lighten the mood. "You're not acting like the other girls."

She finally looked at me, her eyes sharp and piercing. "Listen, I know it's your bachelor party, but I'm not like these other girls."

I smiled, feeling a strange sense of relief. "It's okay. I didn't really want to be here anyway."

For the first time, her expression softened, a tiny smile tugging at the corners of her mouth. She leaned her head back as I poured more oil down her front, her movements deliberate and controlled. She didn't squeeze her chest or shake her hips. She didn't need to. Her presence alone was enough to command the room.

When the bottle was empty, she turned to face Becky, flicking the excess oil off her hands. She shook her head like a bull ready to charge, her fists clenched at her sides.

There was something different about her—something raw and powerful. She wasn't here to put on a show. She was here to fight.

And I believed her when she said she wasn't like the other girls.

Chapter 12

OLIVIA

Before Becky and I even went out to wrestle she kept talking shit about my sister. Saying Emma was a stupid slut, we had no family and shit like that. I was angry but we had to put on a show.

Before Sam introduced me, I watched as Becky put on a strip show for everyone. Then she picked some random dude and gave him a lap dance too. Phone in his pocket? Really? She's disgusting.

Then it was my turn. Sam called my name and I walked to the ring. I didn't strut. I didn't dance. That's not my style. I'm the bouncer and I wrestle. That's it.

Most of the people here know I mean business. Becky might be a show off but I know it's me that everyone came to see.

When Jaxon poured cooking oil on me, he noticed I didn't put on a slut show like Becky or the other girls. I was serious. I looked at this dude and I could see in his eyes that he knew how determined I was.

Strangely enough, he didn't ask me to lie down and roll around in the pit. He didn't ask me to squeeze my tits. He didn't do any of that.

I've been through this a few times before and the dude lucky enough to be my manager for the match, always asks me to squeeze my boobs, then I have to tell him no. This guy just poured the oil on me. Was he shy?

As he kept pouring, he asked, "Is something wrong? You're not acting like those other girls."

I looked at him and said, "Listen, I know it's your bachelor party but I'm not like these other girls."

He smiled, "It's okay, I didn't really want to be here anyway."

My gut feeling told me he was not like all the other horn dogs in this place. I smiled back at him as I leaned my neck back as he poured more oil down my front.

The oil in the ring had pooled into a shallow, glistening puddle, the surface reflecting the harsh stage lights like a distorted mirror. The air was thick with the pungent smell of vegetable oil, a greasy, cloying scent that clung to the back of my throat. It was everywhere—on my skin, in my hair, soaking into the mat beneath me. The slippery, viscous texture made every movement feel exaggerated, like fighting in slow motion. I didn't care. I was done playing nice.

Becky stood across from me, her chest heaving, her body slick and gleaming under the lights. She was smaller than me, her curves accentuated by the oil, but she had a fire in her eyes that I couldn't ignore. Or maybe it was just desperation. Either way, she'd made a mistake. A big one.

Sam's voice boomed through the speakers, cutting through the noise of the crowd. "Are you ready? 3...2...1, let's begin!" *DING!*

The bell rang, and Becky lunged at me, her hands clawing for the straps of my bathing suit. I saw it coming—of course I did—and I grabbed her wrists, twisting them away with a sharp jerk. "What the hell do you think you're doing?" I growled, my voice low and dangerous.

She smirked, her lips curling into a sneer. "Just giving the crowd what they want."

I shoved her back, sending her sprawling into the oil. She landed with a wet *splat*, the sound drowned out by the crowd's cheers.

She wasn't done.

Becky scrambled to her feet, her movements clumsy and uncoordinated, and came at me again. This time, she managed to grab the edge of my top, yanking hard. The fabric stretched, but it didn't give. I smacked her hand away, the sharp crack of my palm against her skin echoing in the room.

"Stop it," I hissed, my voice barely audible over the noise. "You know what I said before!"

She didn't listen. Of course she didn't. She was too busy playing to the crowd, her every move calculated to get a reaction. I thought she knew I wasn't here to play. I was here to win.

I pinned her three times in the first round, each one more forceful than the last. By the time the bell rang, she was breathing hard, her chest rising and falling as she glared at me from across the ring. I could see the frustration in her eyes, the anger bubbling just beneath the surface. Good. Let her be mad. She'd brought this on herself.

During the break, Jaxon handed me a bottle of water, his expression a mix of awe and concern. "This fight is nothing like the first four," he said, his voice low. "You're amazing."

I took the bottle, nodding my thanks. "Yeah, well, she's not making it easy."

He glanced at Becky, who was downing a beer like it was her last meal. "She's… intense."

"You have no idea," I muttered, wiping the oil from my face with a towel. It didn't help much—the greasy residue was everywhere, clinging to my skin like a second layer.

The second round was more of the same. Becky came at me with everything she had, her movements wild and desperate. She tried to pull my top off again, her fingers clawing at the fabric, but I wasn't having it.

I grabbed her arm, twisted it behind her back, and shoved her face into the mat. The crowd roared, their cheers deafening, but I barely heard them. All I could focus on was the rage boiling inside me, the anger that had been building for weeks—no, months.

At the end of round two I was getting angrier and so was she. I stared at her with pure discontent as she gasped for air lying on the mat.

When I rested between round two and three Jaxon gave me another bottle of water and said, "This fight is so much different than the first four. You're…you're incredible."

I gave my water bottle back to him and said, "Thanks."

For me this break was just enough time to catch my breath. I'm sure for Becky this break seemed to only a few seconds.

Becky was still breathing heavy as Sam got on the microphone and asked, "Is everyone ready for the last and final round of the night?"

The cheering was electric. We all said in unison, "YES!"

"Then let the final round begin, now!" DING!

At the beginning of round three, I slid over to her, wrapped my arms around her head and got her in a head lock. She kept wiggling to try and get out of it but she couldn't. My grip was locked in place. I whispered in her ear as she slithered in the slippery substance, "This is a show. Don't try that shit again unless you want to really get hurt."

When the ref made me let her go, she turned around and grabbed my top again. Right between my boobs like a tow truck's hook. She was determined to pull it down as she yelled, "You fuckin freak!"

She didn't pull my suit off because I grabbed her arm, pulled her down and then held my hand on the front of her neck, almost choking her. My wet oily hair dripped in her face as I screamed, "Stop it now!"

She shook her head trying to avoid the Chinese oil torture. At the same time, she flared her legs and wiggled, causing oil to splatter everywhere but she couldn't get away as I held her down.

The ref called this for another pin. "One…two…three!" I was up six to nothing.

The crowd was going wild, their cheers and shouts filling the room, but I barely heard them. All I could focus on was the rage burning inside me.

I got off of her, we separated and as she got away from me, she tried that shit again by pulling the shoulder strap of my suit. What the fuck? Seriously? This time I pulled on her hair and threw her across the ring like I was throwing a bag of garbage in the trash. She slid to the other side of the mat by her corner.

As she was trying to get her balance back, I took a moment and looked at Frank watching from his office door. He was smiling. Almost grinning. He didn't need to twirl his mustache for me to know what was going on.

That was the moment I put two and two together and realized this was a set up. Frank must have talked Becky into trying to rip my clothes off.

At that moment, I was so hot, you could have seen steam coming off my forehead. Feeling pissed things were not going her way Becky stood up, flicked the extra oil off her hands, rushed toward me, and screamed, "Aggghhh!"

Bad idea. I took two steps forward, braced myself and then put my forearm out in front of her. My arm slamming into her chest like a battering ram.

She fell back hard and landed on the mat with a splash. Then I dropped my ass and sat on her chest. She screamed, "Dear God. What the fuck?"

Out of the corner of my eye I saw flashes of light. I assume Jaxon took a picture as I bounced up and down on her stomach and chest to show her how furious I was. Her face flooded with signs of suffering, but I bounced on her again. To her it must have felt like an elephant was using her body like a trampoline. Outraged I yelled, "What's the matter bitch?"

We were in the middle of a wrestling show that was supposed to look like a 'sexy gentleman's club' wrestling match. These people got way more than what they were expecting. Rage flowed through my veins like lava. My anger at her grew inside me like a tumor.

In her somewhat weakened state, I turned her around and interrogated her by bouncing on her back and pulling her arm back as if I wanted to pull it out of its socket, but I couldn't get a good grip because she was so frickin slippery.

I asked, "Was ripping my suit off Frank's idea?"

She screamed with sparks of pain coming out of her voice, "Ahhh…fuck you bitch!"

I tried to turn her over to sit on her chest and pin her again, but she squirmed around like a fish out of water. She did a barrel role and completely spun around. I managed to get her on her stomach again.

This time I drilled my knee in her back and pulled both of her arms back at the same time. She screamed in pain. "Aarggh…get off me!"

The ref made me stop, even though my grip on her arms didn't last long anyway. She was flat on her stomach again, so I straddled her back. I pulled her hair to raise her head up then smacked her in the back of the head.

She lowered her head to get away using her hands up for protection, but I just did the same thing repeatedly. Pull and then smack!

Before I finally got off of her, I pushed her face down in the mat and yelled, "Eat oil bitch!"

When I finally let her go, she scrambled away, her chest heaving, her hands covering her face with was covered with oil. I saw her turn her head toward me, wipe her face like a squeegee and pant for air. Becky was exhausted from getting her ass handed to her, but I wasn't done.

Messing with her face meant she was distracted. I knocked her down again, turned her over on her back, grabbed her leg, raised it as high as it could go and pinned her, again. Sam told everyone, "That makes it eight to zero!"

After the ref counted, Becky managed to slide away from me like a scared blonde bimbo in a horror using her nails to crawl away from her death.

I grabbed her foot and pulled her toward me. "Going somewhere?"

In the next thirty seconds I kicked her ass in the ring over and over. I'm sure to her it seemed like thirty minutes.

It started when I pulled her greasy hair again. She reached around to try and grab my hair too, but I shook her head up and down four or five times.

Then I used her hair as a pully, flipping her over. She landed with a splash. When she hit the plastic mat, I slapped her with a few hard hits to her bare stomach. She reached up to try and pull my hair, to get me to stop but I grabbed her thigh, slid my hand all the way down to her ankle, clutched on to it as tight as I could and pulled her foot up to her head. Slippery or not, she wasn't moving! This was pin number nine.

After a while she didn't fight back anymore, all she wanted to do was get away from me. She screamed, "You're fucking crazy bitch!"

She tried to walk out of the ring and give up, but I pulled her back to me by grabbing the back of her bathing suit as if it was a handle.

She cried out, "Stop this crazy bitch!" To shut her up I wrapped my arms around her whole body and squeezed. Since my arms were long and she was a lot shorter than me all she could move was her legs. Dripping with slippery oil didn't matter. Her arms were locked in my grip, and she couldn't move. It was like I was trying to squeeze a big wet water balloon.

I turned my head for a second to see Jaxon taking a picture of this. The crowd loved how aggressive it got. The enthusiasm from everyone grew increasingly. It was one of the best wrestling shows they ever had at the club.

Just as it was about to end, she tried to pull my bathing suit down one last time. Her index finger looped under my strap.

Are you fucking kidding? Hasn't she had enough?

The rage rose through me like a tsunami. I swung my arm around like I wanted to hit a home run and smacked her in the face, again. The wetness on our bodies made the sound echo in the room.

SMACK!

Becky laid on the mat holding her face, on the verge of passing out. I didn't care anymore. She was too weak to fight back as I pulled her up by her hair. Her arms dangled to her side like limp noodles. It was like I was a hunter showing off my kill.

Jaxon snapped another picture as I yelled to Frank, "Hey, Frank! Your bitch failed. You will never see me naked in this fuckin bar, got it!"

Frank looked a little irritated. The audience thought this was all part of the show. They loved seeing me, the big, tall woman, beat the crap out of someone small. This is what Frank wanted and this is what the audience wanted. This is what they got.

With my other hand I unsnapped Becky's bikini top and pulled it off, yelling to the audience, "Is this what you wanted to see? Tits? Because you're not going to see mine."

I gave Becky's top and few solid swings and threw it into the audience. It was like throwing food to starving carp. These pervs didn't care if it was soaked in used cooking oil, they wanted a cool souvenir.

Then pushed Becky down on the mat. She collapsed on the plastic pit like she was about to lose consciousness. Her body stopped where she landed and didn't move. Her eye barely up and she looked at me from a defeated position. Maybe she knew now that whatever deal she had with Frank wasn't worth it. I just kicked her ass and humiliated her in front of everyone.

Just before the last round ended, I dropped my body down and knelt on Becky's shoulders. I had her pinned with her head locked between my legs. Our bodies were slick, but I used my strong legs like a vice and squeezed her head like I was trying to pop a watermelon with my thighs. I felt drunk with rage.

With her head locked between my legs I grabbed her hair so she couldn't move her head at all. My fist was clenched as solid as a rock, and I was about to punch her in the face for the stunt she tried to pull with Frank.

She looked truly scared with her head locked between my crotch. I could see the terror in her eyes. She thought I was going to punch her and hurt her very badly. Her black mascara makeup was running down her face which reminded me of a racoon. I couldn't tell if she was crying or if she was just a mess, which we both were.

She mustered up what strength she had left and flared her legs up and down over and over, but she still couldn't move that much. She tried to use her arms to reach up and push me off, but her arms were not long enough to do anything. They fell to her side like a dead weight.

Now was my chance. My blood was boiling, and I wanted to fuck her up good.

But I didn't.

I thought about how my dad used to beat me and my sister with the belt. I thought about how my mom was in jail. I needed to be there for my sister. If I beat the living shit out of Becky, she might try to press charges.

So, I kept my frustration in check. Instead of punching her in the face with no mercy, I punched the mat right next to her face. Just before the bell rang to end round three, and to finally bring this beat down to an end, I held her shoulders down and pinned her…again. For the tenth time.

Sam said, "With a win of 10 to 0, your champion wrestler at the Rat Hole and still undefeated – The Queen Bee."

The crowd went nuts. Becky had lost - big time! Before I got up to let Becky go, I pointed to Jaxon by my side. "Hey, you, it's your bachelor party, I won. Take a picture of this."

He took his cell phone out and snapped a picture again. Beckey's head locked between my legs as I flexed my arms up. Then I said to him, "Sorry you didn't get to see my boobs. Like I said before, I'm not like those other girls."

As Becky lay there breathing heavy, I finally got up, put my foot on her stomach and waived to the audience. I felt like a true champion showing to everyone that I beat this bitch. She was beneath me and most important my clothes were still on.

As she slowly got up, I shoved her out of the ring and forced her to do the 'walk of shame.' Only this time all the degrading comments I yelled were from the heart. I really hated this bitch, "Go on. Do the walk of shame, bitch! Frank wants his dick sucked. Don't forget to swallow you stupid fucking slut."

She stumbled through the crowd, her head lowered, her body trembling as the crowd jeered and laughed. I watched her go, my chest heaving, my fists clenched at my sides. I couldn't really tell if she was playing this part up for the audience or if her humiliating walk felt real to her this time because I kicked her ass so bad.

The crowd went ape shit for this because they thought the banter was part of the show. It always was but this time, I really meant it.

The rage was still there, simmering beneath the surface, but I'd held back. I hadn't crossed the line. Not yet.

I stood there, in the ring, still a dripping oily mess, the crowd's cheers ringing in my ears, I couldn't help but wonder how much longer I could keep it together.

Chapter 13

JAXON

This night turned out to be something I never expected. It was supposed to be a night out with friends from work. Girls shake their ass, and we go home. It was far from that.

I can't believe I was bored from the first four matches of the night. The last match made this whole night worth the wait. It was a great – WRESTLING – match!

When I saw this tall woman, with long legs, long arms and all wet and sloppy from the oil, wrap her arms around the other girl and squeeze, she looked like a large Kraken wrapping its tentacles around a ship at sea.

Noa was right. This was the one I was looking for. The one big client my girlfriend told me about. I saw a star!

When the match was over, before she got up, she pointed to me and said, "Hey you, it's your bachelor party, get your phone out and take a picture of this."

I took my cell phone out and snapped a picture of The Queen Bee's victory. A few strands of wet hair flopped in front of her face when she flexed her arms up. Her whole body shined and glistened in the stage lights as the loser's head was locked between this giant woman's legs.

Then she said to me, "Sorry you didn't get to see my boobs. Like I said before, I'm not like those other girls."

When The Queen Bee finally got off of her, she yelled some humiliating and degrading comments as the girl she defeated walked to an office. As all this was happening, I looked at my 'bachelor party' photo of this very tall woman, a hot wet mess, flexing with a smile on her face that exuded a satisfying win. There's no denying she looked hot and amazing, but I didn't see anything sexual. I saw a champion.

When The Queen Bee walked off stage, I tried to get her attention, but she walked away too fast.

Sam asked me as I was getting up, "What did you think Jaxon?"

He put the mic in front of my face as I answered, "That was an amazing fight."

"One of the best wrestling matches we've ever had here at the Rat Hole."

While he kept rambling on, I got up off the stage and saw our waitress Mary Ann. I knew it was her because she was the only girl in here with a cowboy hat on, "Hey, what was that tall girl's name?"

She told me, "The Queen Bee."

I knew it was her stage name, so I asked again, "No, her real name."

"I'm sorry sweety. As far as you know, she's the Queen Bee."

I saw the dancer Coco coming out from back stage. Her hair was still a little wet. She must had just gotten out of the shower. I asked her the same question and she told me the same thing too. None of them would tell me her real name.

My friends called me back to our table.

I asked them, "Did you guys happen to see where that tall woman went?"

Rick snickered, "Probably to go take a shower. She's a fucking mess."

Jerry being the ass hat that he is asked, "Dude, can you send me some of those pictures?"

"Not now, Jerry."

It didn't matter what they were saying because I couldn't stop thinking about the Queen Bee. Her tallness, her toughness. I had to talk to her to find out more about her.

I had to know who she was.

Unfortunately, now was not the time.

Chapter 14

OLIVIA

The clock had just struck 1 a.m., and the wrestling show was over. The stage area reeked of stale beer, sweat, and the faint, greasy smell of old cooking oil—like a fast-food joint shutting down for the night. The bar was nearly empty, save for a few stragglers nursing their drinks. The dim, flickering lights cast long shadows across the sticky floor, and the air felt heavy, almost suffocating, as if the walls themselves were closing in.

I had just showered, scrubbing away the grime and the lingering stench of the ring, but no amount of soap could wash away the anger boiling inside me. Frank had crossed a line tonight, and I was done. I stormed toward his office, my boots thudding against the wooden floor, my fists clenched so tight my nails dug into my palms. The adrenaline still coursed through me, hot and electric, like a live wire sparking in the dark.

When I reached his office, the door was locked. Of course it was. I smirked bitterly, muttering under my breath, "Bet some girl's earning her bonus." Without hesitation, I reared back and kicked the door with everything I had. The wood splintered around the lock, and the door flew open with a deafening crack.

"Frank, you asshole!" I shouted; my voice sharp enough to cut glass. "Why did you have Becky—"

I froze mid-sentence. There he was, Frank, sitting in his chair, his face a mask of shock. His cell phone was in his hand, the screen casting a harsh, unnatural glow across the room.

Then I saw her—Becky, rising from her knees in front of him, wiping her mouth with the back of her hand. Her skin on her naked body glistened under the dim light, oily and slick. The smell of her cheap perfume mixed with the acrid stench of sweat, vegetable oil and something else I didn't want to name.

I was in shock, "Are you fucking shitting me? This whole 'walk of shame' shit was real?"

"What the fuck?" Frank barked, his voice cracking. "I thought I locked that door!"

"You did," I snapped, my tone dripping with sarcasm. "I opened it."

Becky glared at me, her eyes blazing with defiance. "You could've killed me out there, you crazy bitch!"

"Me?" I shot back, my voice rising. "Who's the one sucking the boss's cock because you lost?"

She sneered, crossing her arms over her chest. "You're the only one who hasn't."

"Yeah, because I'm the only one with any fucking decency!" I spat, my hands trembling with rage.

She smirked, "It doesn't matter if I lost. I already got paid."

"Wait—did this sleazeball actually pay you to try and rip my clothes off?"

Frank's face went pale. "What? No! I would never—"

"A grand," Becky interrupted, her lips curling into a smug smile.

Frank groaned, slumping back in his chair. "Shit."

"A grand?" I repeated, my voice low and dangerous. "You paid her a grand to humiliate me?"

I snarled at Becky, "Yet, I still beat the living shit out of you and to top it off you still had to suck…"

It suddenly hit me. My sister and I wrestled too, "Oh my God, my sister. She lost too."

Frank's lips twitched into a smirk, and that was it. That was the final straw. "That woman has no gag reflex," he said, his voice dripping with disdain.

Something inside me snapped. The room seemed to shrink, the air thickening with the weight of my fury. I lunged at him, grabbing him by the collar and yanking him out of his chair. His eyes widened in fear, and for the first time, I saw the coward behind the bravado. His pulse raced under my grip, his breath coming in shallow gasps as I slammed him against the wall.

"You think this is funny?" I growled, my voice low and venomous. "You think it's okay to use these girls—to use my sister—like they're nothing?"

Becky grabbed at my sides, trying to pull me away, but I barely felt her. I was a force of nature, unstoppable and unrelenting. I grabbed a fistful of her greasy hair and shoved her aside, sending her stumbling to the floor. She landed with a thud, her cries of protest fading into the background as I focused on Frank.

I didn't hold back. My knee drove into his groin with a sickening crunch, and he doubled over, his face contorted in agony. My fist followed, connecting with his cheekbone so hard I felt the impact reverberate up my arm. His nose crunched under the force, blood spurting as he crumpled to the floor.

The room was a blur of motion and sound—Frank's groans, Becky's whimpers, the metallic smell of blood in the air. I kicked him again, my boot connecting with his ribs, and he curled into a ball, his hands clutching his stomach.

"I want to kill you so fucking bad," I hissed, my voice shaking with barely contained rage. "But I won't. Not tonight. Consider this your punishment for being the piece of shit you are."

Becky scrambled to her feet, her face pale and tear-streaked. "I'm going to make sure he sues you!" she screeched.

I laughed, a harsh, bitter sound. "Go ahead. I'm a bouncer at a strip bar. What's he gonna take? My dignity? Oh wait—I still have that. Unlike you."

Frank groaned, blood dribbling from his nose as he struggled to sit up. "You...I...oh fuck."

"What's the matter, Frank?" I taunted, crouching down to his level. "Did I break a rib? Good. Maybe it'll remind you not to mess with me—or my sister—ever again."

He nodded weakly, his eyes pleading for mercy. I grabbed his hair, forcing him to look at me. "If anything happens to her, I'll come back for you. I'll make sure your face will look like raw hamburger meat. Got it?"

He nodded his head. We had an agreement.

I released him, and he slumped to the floor, a broken, pathetic mess. Becky stared at me; her defiance replaced by fear. I wiped my hands on my jeans, the greasy residue from her hair making my skin crawl. "Take a shower, Becky," I muttered. "You smell like a dead fish."

As I walked out of the office, the door hanging precariously on its hinges, I felt a strange sense of relief.

I left the bar and rain had started to fall outside, the cool droplets washing over me as I stepped into the night. It was as if the world itself was cleansing me of the filth I'd endured for far too long.

I didn't look back. The Rat Hole was behind me now, and so was Frank. For the first time in a long time, I felt free.

As I walked to Emma's car, I thought to myself, '*I really need my own car now that I'm not working in the same place as Emma.*'

After all that happened tonight, I finally checked my phone and saw that I got a text from Emma about an hour ago.

I'm entertaining.

Could you wait to come home?

Sorry I responded late.

Trouble at the Rat hole.

Tell me about it laterrr.

Bussyyy.

Her text was weird, I asked…

R U doing drugs? R U drunk?

No

Fine. U have 2 hours.

Only 2?

I'm tired. I want to go to bed.

I'll be home at 4am.

k

After I left the bar, I went out for a late-night breakfast.

It just so happened that the guy who poured oil on me when I wrestled was there too.

He saw me and I looked at him, but I wasn't paying too much attention to him because I thought he was just another creep who went to strip bars. He was here with his buddies. An after-bachelor party breakfast I suppose.

Chapter 15

JAXON

After the party, close to 1 a.m., all of us guys went out to breakfast at a local mom & pop place out in the middle of nowhere called Aunt Millie's. Very quaint place. It looked like it hadn't been updated in thirty years but the food was fantastic. Eggs cooked to perfection, waffles were lightly sweet and airy and the sausage tasted fresh.

Jerry was plastered so Evan took him home while Rick and I finished up our late-night breakfast.

I confessed to Rick as we ate, "You know, I texted Noa a few times while we were there."

"You got reception down there?"

"It was slow but yeah, I did. After watching the first four matches I told her I was bored."

"Bored?"

"They weren't really wrestling, were they?"

"No, but that's part of the bachelor party experience. Touching and feeling, slipping and sliding without actually doing the deed in front of everyone."

I took a sip of my coffee and added, "That last girl put on a hell of a show."

"Oh yeah. She was awesome!"

No sooner than five minutes after Evan and Jerry left, and Rick and I started talking about her, I saw her come in. That tall girl. The Queen Bee. Maybe Noa was right. The universe is letting me know what I need. What are the odds that I saw a very tall woman wrestler for my bachelor party and now she's also here, at the same restaurant where I had breakfast with my friends.

I told Rick, "There she is."

"Who?"

"That super tall girl."

"What? You're kidding? We were just taking about her."

I know it's not polite to stare but I watched as she came in the restaurant. Her hair was wet and she had a light shine to her skin. She talked to the hostess, and sat on the far end of the room.

I looked at Rick and asked, "Honest opinion, do you think she'd make a great wrestler?"

He smiled, "After what we saw her do, hell yea. She'd make a great wrestler." Then his smiled changed.

He added, "Then again, she does work in a strip bar. You know John's policy on no nudes. As long as she's never taken off her clothes in that…"

I looked at him as he talked. Then he stopped. It was like a telepathic communication. He knew what I was thinking as I smiled. "Go talk to her. I'll wait in the car."

I got up and headed in her direction. He whispered, "Good luck."

I walked closer to her slowly. Out of the corner of my eye I saw Rick pay our bill and walk out. Then, I walked up to her table and asked, "Hi. Remember me?"

Sarcastically she responded, "The bachelor party guy who dumped vegetable oil all over me? Jaxon, is it?"

Sensing some aggression, I tried again but softer. "Yeah, that's me."

"I guess the pictures of me kicking that girl's ass wasn't enough?"

I tend to ramble when I get excited, "No, that was great. You were great. The show was fantastic. My name is Jaxon Anderson. I'm a sports promoter for Westman Sports Agency. Can we talk?"

"Talk…about what?"

I took a breath and confessed, "This is going to sound crazy, but my fiancé believes everything happens for a reason. She believes in karma, yin-and-yang and all that cosmic stuff. Most of the time I think she's crazy, but I love her and respect her."

"As you should if you're going to marry her. What does that have to do with me?"

"This time, she was right."

"What?"

I wanted to sit down but I didn't because this girl was staring me down like a wild cat about to strike its prey, so I waited for her to invite me to sit, "Here me out first. I love sports. I wanted to go fishing or to a sports show for my bachelor party but my 'soon to be wife' insisted that I go out with the guys."

Olivia gave me a look, "Insisted?"

"Yes, insisted. Remember what I told you back at the bar? I didn't really want to be there anyway."

She nodded her head as I continued, "I didn't want to go but I did. And low-and-behold at this bar, I met - you! That can't be a coincidence. Now before you send me away for acting like a creep…"

Olivia looked at me and cracked a smile, "I don't think you're a creep. You didn't act like all the other drunk horny guys who oil up the girls. I could tell you were different."

I was relieved, "Good."

"You're not going to sneak away and jack off to those pictures you took of me when your fiancé isn't looking are you?"

"What? No. My fiancé is the best woman in the world. If you want me to, I can delete them all right now."

She smiled, "That won't be necessary. You seem like a decent guy. You don't give me creepy vibes. Have a seat Jaxon. I'm Olivia."

"Thank you."

She asked, "I still don't understand why you want to talk to me? Thanks to my sleezy boss I'm still a God-awful mess and I probably smell like a French Fry."

I tried to lighten the mood, "You look fine, really."

She gave me a sarcastic look.

"Alright, truth is you don't smell bad, but you could use a shower."

"You see, that's the thing. I took two showers already."

"Oh, I'm sorry. I just assumed because your hair was so wet, and your body was still glistening you didn't."

"Dude, it's raining out."

I felt bad, "Again, my bad. Sorry. I'm going to get right to the point. I think you could be a pro wrestler."

She threw her head back with her forehead scrunched up, "What? A pro wrestler? Are you insane? I looked like a freak out there tonight."

"No, you looked determined. Those other girls put on a sexy show. You didn't. All you wanted to do was kick her ass."

She said as her anger grew, "After what she tried to pull, you're damn right." Then took a sip of her coffee.

"You see. That's what I'm talking about. Feisty and gritty."

Olivia was still undecided, "I don't know. I've always thought my tallness made me look like a monster. I only used my size to my advantage as the bouncer to keep an eye on my sister at that stupid bar. I was dumb enough to let Frank talk me into wrestling."

"You're not dumb."

"Yes, I am. Those guys looked at me like I was some sort of sex object. It gives me the creeps knowing all those guys will probably go home and crank one out thinking about what I did to Becky."

"I assume that comes with the territory when working in an establishment like that, doesn't it?"

She lifted her toast about to take a bite but stopped, "Maybe, but I was the fucking bouncer! I had respect. Now I'm just the tall freak who wrestled. Nobody is going to take me seriously as a professional wrestler if my career started off in a pit of ten gallons of cooking oil."

"A freak? No. You're a star."

She rolled her eyes, "Whatever."

I could see she needed more convincing, "No matter how much you hated what you did in that pit tonight, it helped me see what you're made of. It showed me you have what it takes to fight and put on a show."

"You're starting to sound like Frank. He said I could put on a good show, but I felt – fake. That whole 'walk of shame' thing was his idea."

"Humiliating the loser? Almost sounds like a pro wrestling match."

I sensed a bit of aggression in her voice, "No, what's humiliating is I let Frank talk me into embarrassing myself as a fucking oil and mud wrestler in that place. I'm done putting on a show. I think I'll pass."

Shit, I'm losing her. "Before you send me away, let me ask you, what are your stats? That DJ, Sam, he didn't exaggerate about you, did he?"

"No. I'm six foot six, and just over two hundred pounds."

I got excited. She is so perfect. I tried to convince her more, "Professional wrestling is better than working at a strip club."

Olivia went into a long-winded speech defending her friends and her sister, "Listen, every strip club is different, but I think some of them get a bad name."

"What? Really?""

"Yes. Some guys go to strip clubs just to talk to someone because their wives won't listen to them. It's their therapy."

I was blown away by this information, "I had no idea."

"No. I'm serious. I remember Amber told me some guy paid her a hundred bucks for a private lap dance. Her dance was cut short because all he really wanted was someone to listen to him. It was cheaper than going to a shrink."

"I never thought about a strip club that way."

"Plus, there's the money too. Now I admit my sister strips because she likes to party and there is some drug use in there from time to time. Oh, and Frank's a real creepy asshole but some girls strip because it's a way to make a quick buck."

There we go. Now this is what the typical strip clubs sounds like to me. Money.

She continued, "Why would she work at a fast-food place making fifteen dollars an hour when she can make five hundred a night taking off her clothes? Some of the smart ones use a fan site on the internet to make a killing and the strip club is a place you can meet them in person. Again, every strip club is different. The Rat Hole just happened to be your typical strip club with serious stuff going on but they're not all like that, so I've heard."

"And you? Are you one of those who also took their clothes off?"

She answered very sternly. "Oh, hell no! I never took my clothes off. Like I said I was the bouncer. Frank, the owner of that shit hole, convinced me I would be the one wrestler all the guys would want to see, and he was right. I made over a thousand dollars every time I wrestled. That was until he tried to make one of his bitches rip my clothes off. So, as you saw up close, I kicked her ass."

"That you did."

She sighed, "Now I don't work there anymore. I quit."

She needs a job? Oh, come on, this is meant to be, "So, you're free then."

"Yes, but I don't know. Professional wrestling sounds more complicated. I might get hurt."

I took a deep breath and told her, "It's true. You could get hurt but with your size I'd be more worried about YOU hurting them."

That comment made her smile. I continued as I pulled out my phone, "Besides, a lot of wrestling is for show, a performance."

"That's what Frank said about oil wrestling until I found out Becky was paid to try and rip my clothes off."

"I take it beating the crap out of her and humiliating her wasn't part of the show?"

Olivia expressed with a pinch of anger, "No. That was all me being super pissed at her. She deserved that beating!"

I continued, "Listen, Frank was somewhat right. Wrestling is partly a performance, but you also need to train your body to take a hit. The show — the performance - is the banter before and after the fight and sometimes during, the 'wrestling' is real. Here are a few of my former clients."

The first picture that popped up was the one of Olivia with her arms flexing in the oil pit.

She gave me a sarcastic look. I take it she didn't really want to see that, "What? It was the last picture I took."

She rolled her eyes, "I hope I never see that again."

I swiped through all the pics I took of Olivia and eventually got to my former clients, "Anyway, this is Heather."

Olivia's eyes raised a little. Then I showed her more, "This is Flora."

"She looks bitchy."

"She was and not just in the ring either."

"I get it. That's enough."

"Are you sure? I have video too."

"No, I don't need to see anymore."

I put my phone down and told her, "I can totally see you as someone like these girls, but better! I know you can do it."

"You really think so?"

"Yes, you're the tallest female wrestler I've ever seen. You're like Andre the Giant but female. You're powerful, you can get angry and thanks to what I saw tonight, I know you can fight."

Olivia took a sip of her water, "Will I ever have to oil or mud wrestle again? Because I really don't want to, ever."

"Never! I do professional wrestling. Female oil and mud wrestling in a bar is a sexy show. When I saw you wrestling tonight, I had a feeling …no – I KNEW you didn't belong there. I knew you could be so much more."

I finally got through to her. She responded with a smile, "Okay, I'll do it, but I refuse to wear high heels. I can't stand them. Besides, I'm already tall enough."

I laughed a little, "I can work with that."

Chapter 16

OLIVIA

I came home to my apartment at 4:30am. The rain had stopped but it was still very wet out. Almost as if the rain was like a shower that washed away the dirt and grime.

I was about to open the lobby door when a man I'd never seen before opened it for me. He was bald and it was hard not to notice he had a snake tattoo on his neck that ran up his cheek and into his ear.

He was surprised to see me standing in front of him. "Sorry, oh…wait. Olivia?"

"Yes, how do you know who I am?"

"Emma said she knew The Queen Bee and I saw you wrestle tonight at The Rat Hole. That was an incredible fight! Plus, there's not that many women your height around here."

"Point taken." Then I started to walk in, but he stopped me, "Hey, you can oil wrestle me anytime."

What an asshole. The first time I saw this guy he hits on me, and he expects me to fight him? "Dude, you saw what I did to that girl. If I kicked your ass, you wouldn't survive."

"Sounds like a wonderful way to go. Death by…"

I rolled my eyes and ignored his comment, "Whoever you are, good night."

He strolled away with a strut thinking he was cool.

When I walked in my apartment, I immediately noticed the funky smell of sweat and sex. My sister was still up walking around the place topless and smiling.

She brought up my appearance and smell right away, "Whoa, you smell weird."

"Me? It's this apartment. Why does this place smell like twelve hairy men spent an hour in a sauna? Did you have an orgy in here?"

Her cheeks glowed as she responded, "Close. Not twelve, just two. Only one was hairy."

As I walked to the window my hands and head quivered. My tongue rolled out of my mouth trying my best not to throw up as I pictured a hairy sweaty man in my apartment.

I opened a window to air out the place as she asked, "Don't you usually take a shower after you wrestle?"

I shot her a look, "I did."

"Oh. Why is your hair still wet and you smell like fried chicken?"

I huffed, "For your information, it was raining out and Frank used vegetable oil instead of baby oil tonight."

She laughed, "Oh. You might want to shower again before you go to bed."

"Fuck off!"

"I already did, multiple times."

I closed my eyes and raised my hand, "Shut up, I don't want to hear it."

She was holding a glass of wine, so I asked, "Where did my nineteen-year-old underage sister get alcohol?"

"They bought it for me."

"They?"

"Yeah, my company just left."

"Was that snake face doing a walk of shame?"

Emma smiled with delight, "Walk of shame? Oh hell no. There's a reason he has a snake tattoo. His cock is as big as a…"

I walked away, to the kitchen, as my nose wrinkled and my stomach felt nauseated, "Shut up. I don't want you to finish that sentence!"

"Fine. You get the point anyway."

I pulled a bottle of water out of the fridge, "Yes, I do. That must be why you're letting the girls air out then."

Emma smiled shaking the top half of her body, "Yeah. They needed some time off from all the squeezing, poking, and caressing."

My eyes rolled, "That's enough. I don't need to know the details."

She pressed one of her boobs as she said, "Snake face, as you call him, suggested I get a boob job."

"What? Why? You have a perfect thirty-eight C cup."

"They're only a thirty-two-C and I happen to think he might be right. Bigger boobs would get me more attention."

I sat down in front of her and said, "The wrong kind of attention is a bad thing, trust me."

"I know but if I had bigger tits the customers would pay more attention to me. If the eyes of all the guys were drawn to me, I'd make more money. You're so tall your huge knockers don't look that big on you."

I almost spit out the water I was drinking, "Huge? Really?"

"Yes, huge! Why do you think Frank wanted you to wrestle? He was hoping your suit would slip off. He wanted to see your tits so fucking bad."

My lips tightened and curled as my eyebrows knitted in anger, "Oh my God. That was his plan the whole time? I hate him even more now. Why didn't you tell me?"

"I thought it was obvious."

I took a deep breath and told her what happened, "Enough boob talk. Look, Emma, I need to tell you something important."

"What?"

"I quit the club tonight."

"Why?"

"Frank is the biggest asshole I've ever seen. He paid Becky to try and rip my clothes off when we wrestled."

Emma looked surprised, "I knew, remember, but holy shit, that's low. Did she succeed?"

"Hell no, I kicked her ass."

"Serves her right then to mess with my big sister." She took a sip of wine smiling with pride.

That made me smile too, "Thanks."

Then I continued, "Good thing is, I got my biggest tip ever from a bachelor party before I quit. One of the guys in his party paid two grand to make sure the guy named Jaxon poured oil on me."

"Holy shit! Two thousand dollars?"

"Yeah. I about flipped my shit."

"Why the hell did you quit? Look at the kind of money you could make."

I closed my eyes and sighed, "It wasn't worth the price of my dignity anymore. I'm going to save it because I'm sure I'll need it later now that I don't have a job."

"True."

I looked at my sister deeply concerned, "After Becky lost, I took a shower and ran into Frank's office to tell him I was quitting but found Becky giving our boss a blowjob. He was recording it on his cell phone."

Emma wasn't fazed by this information, "Yeah, so."

"Emma, we wrestled, you lost."

"Yeah, so."

I couldn't believe what I just heard. "Are you fucking kidding me? Emma, he's your boss. That's sexual harassment. Did he video you too?"

"Yes, he did. Frank has this thing for sexy, wet, shiny girls giving him head. Something about wet hair and a shiny face. That's why he loves oil wrestling so much. He paid me as an actress in his short film."

Oh my God. I couldn't believe my ears. "Emma, you have to leave that place, Frank is a sleaze ball."

"I don't want to leave. I like it there. I make good money and I meet nice people."

"Nice people like snake face?"

"He has a name you know. It's Tate. No wait, that was the first guy. Tate called his friend who was at the Rat Hole."

I closed my eyes and threw my face into my hand. I couldn't believe what she just said, "I don't care what his name is, he has a tattoo - on his face! It's very…wait a minute, was Tate the third guy?"

"No. Just two. Tonight, I experienced my first threesome."

"Never mind. I don't need to know details."

Emma smiled a mischievous grin as she took a drink of her wine. "You should try it sometime. You might like it."

"No thank you."

Then I continued, "Listen, you're old enough to make your own decisions. I'm worried about you, that's all."

"That's sweet. Thanks."

"I met someone too."

"Oh, does he have a big cock like the snake man?"

My eyes widened, "Seriously? Is that all you ever think about?"

"What?"

"I don't know how big his dick is and I don't want to know. Remember the guy I told you about, Jaxon?"

"Yeah."

"He's actually a sports promoter. He wants to help me be a professional wrestler."

My sister's eyelids lit up by this news, "For real? A professional wrestler?"

"Yeah."

"You have the size. That's for sure."

I looked deep at my sister, "It seems like a great opportunity for me but again I'm worried about you."

"Why?"

"You're my little sister. I only got the job at that hole in the ground place because I wanted to keep an eye on you."

"Aww…you care."

"Of course, I do. Remember that time that drunk toothless dude kept grabbing you?"

Emma's face expelled disgust, "Yes, and might I add, yuk!"

"Who threw him out?"

She smiled, "You did."

"What about Vick the old guy with the hairy chest and receding hair line?"

A smile grew on her face, "Oh yeah, he was an ass but damn he was also so flippin cute too."

"Cute? The guy was hitting sixty and walking with a cane. That's what I'm talking about Emma. You're so distracted by sex you can't see who's using you and who is actually a nice guy."

She looked away as she said, "Nice guys are boring."

"Most of the ones you find attractive are assholes. They just want to use you." My words went unnoticed.

Emma said with a flirty smile as she put her finger on her lower lip, "Frank's kinda cute for an older guy too. Like a sexy dad. Does he have kids?"

I screamed as my hands shook in frustration at her, "He's the worst! He uses all his girls for sex. Emma, I really want you to leave that place, but I know you'd be pissed at me if I got Frank in trouble for hiring girls who aren't old enough to be there."

Emma got a little angry, "Yes, I would. I make great money there. Besides, Frank didn't use me, I used him. I got paid as an actress. Two hundred bucks for one flipping blowjob. That's a steal."

I couldn't believe what she just said. Doesn't she know he's going to use the video of her and make ten times more than what he paid her from the views of the video? Plus, once it hits the porn sites it's out there, forever.

I took a breath to calm down, "I'm just saying, I'm not going to be there anymore to look after you, so I let him know, in a very persuasive way, never to mess with us again."

She looked puzzled.

Then I told her, "He said some shit about you, and I finally had enough of all the crap he was pulling to get the girls to suck his cock. So, I let him know it was wrong, in my own way."

The surprised look on her face was priceless, "What?"

"I beat the shit out of Frank, aright!"

A tinge of panic set in, "Aren't you afraid he's going to come after you?"

"Not really. We…well, we have an agreement."

"Do tell."

"There's nothing to tell. Just know he won't bother us anymore."

"Bother us?"

"Yes, us. Well, me for sure since I don't work there anymore. If he starts shit with you just say, 'I'm going to give my sister a call.' He'll probably cower and cry in the corner like you just took a little girl's doll away and give you whatever you want."

She laughed and said, "I will" as she drank down her last swallow of wine.

I told her, "I'm tired. I'm going to bed. I have to be at the gym Monday at 8 a.m. Which reminds me, since we don't work in the same place anymore, I'll need your car on Monday."

"That's fine. I'm still sleeping at that time anyway."

I walked to my room and added, "I'll start looking for a new car soon."

"So, you're going to sleep all day tomorrow?"

"No, but I am going to get a good night's rest. I have no idea what's in store for me now."

As I closed the door to my room, I whispered to myself, "And neither do you."

Chapter 17

JAXON

Early Monday morning I opened the doors to my fiancé's gym, Home Town Fitness. Noa's parents helped her buy this place a few years ago. Yoga, Zumba classes, weights, treadmills, steppers and recently added a wrestling ring for me and my clients. She's been doing very well with this place. I bring my wrestlers here to train.

There's a small office for her brother who manages the business, but he had today off. So, since I bring so many clients here, today it's my office.

I turned on the lights and I could still smell the aroma of sweat. She has this place cleaned every night but no matter how much bleach or cleaner they use, every morning there's always some lingering odor of a high school boys locker room.

Around 7:30 the trainer I hired, Josh Nickels, came in. He's a big dude who's trained all my wrestlers. I've been working with him ever since I started at Westman. "Good morning, Josh."

"Mornin'."

He took a sip of his protein shake and asked, "So where's this new wrestler of yours?"

"She'll be in soon."

I walked away to go to the bathroom, and he yelled, "How will I know who she is?"

I laughed, "Trust me. You won't be able to miss her. She's my next big star."

If it wasn't obvious, I didn't tell him how tall Olivia was before he met her.

Just before Olivia came in, I sat on the shitter looking at my phone and watched a video of Flora on YouTube. She was now going by 'Foxy Krush.' I sighed and said, "Foxy Krush. That's a good name." I watched how she was talking smack about her upcoming match. I knew she was all talk, but I couldn't help but sigh and feel a little disappointed she got away.

Just as I was finishing up washing my hands, I heard Josh scream, "Holy Shit."

I chuckled as I walked out of the bathroom and said, "I see you met Olivia."

"When you said she was your next big star you weren't kidding. Where did you find this one?"

"Actually, I saw her at my bachelor party."

Olivia yelled and stopped me from going any further, "Hey, I'd rather forget about that place."

"Alright, Josh, it doesn't matter where I found her, have you ever trained someone her size before?"

"Men this size all the time but a female this tall, no. It shouldn't be too difficult though."

I asked Olivia, "How fast do you want to reach the goal of your first match? Average training time is three months to one year. Fast or slow?"

Olivia responded, "The quicker the better. I don't have a job now, remember."

"Good, I was hoping you'd say that. Three months of intense training it is. I hope you can take the training. If you can, it will pay off quick for you and me."

Before we begin, I told her, "Let's head to the office to get you started. Paperwork and boring stuff. You said you were around two hundred pounds, right?"

We walked and talked and as we entered the office she answered, "Around there."

"That's the average size of a six-foot six female. You're not fat but you're not wrestler size. I'd like you to be more than just average. I want you to bulk up a little. Maybe hit two hundred twenty-five or two thirty."

She felt insulted, "Sounds like you want me to be fat."

We both sat down as I said, "No…no. You have the wrong idea. I want you to be all muscle. Leaner and more toned."

"Okay, I see what you're saying."

"You'll need to cut certain foods like sugar and high fat foods from your diet. No bread, no sweets, and eat more lean protein and vegetables. I want you to consume about 3,500 – 4,000 calories a day but it has to be good healthy food. Do this, along with some weightlifting, and you'll see your body will slowly take shape."

Just then I got a surprise visit from my soon to be wife Noa who popped into the office. She wanted to see Olivia for herself. I told Noa, "Hi honey. This is Olivia."

Noa looked at Olivia, "Stand up for me. I want to see just how tall you are."

Olivia stood up and she towered over my poor fiancé. That didn't matter. Noa closed her eyes and waved her hands in front of Olivia's body as if she was casting evil spirits away. "I sense a positive aura around you but…you've been hurt. Your strength and power are a defense for something else."

"Noa, please. I'm trying to get her started with wrestling."

Olivia waved her hand at me, "No, wait. Let her finish."

They didn't see me, but I rolled my eyes, "All-right."

Noa breathed a few deep breaths and then opened her eyes, "You're strong - because you need to be."

I tried to explain to Noa what I felt about Olivia, "I've seen firsthand that she can be immensely powerful when she learns to harness her anger. The problem is controlling that anger and using it in the ring."

"What do you mean? I didn't hurt her that bad."

I raised one eyebrow and said, "You pulled her up by her hair like a dead animal."

She smiled, "True. Well, you also don't know this but after you left, I did kick the crap out of Frank, but he deserved it. He was a creep."

Noa looked deep into Olivia's eyes and said, "You need to figure out what you're mad at. Have you tried meditation?"

Olivia answered, "Never."

"Maybe you should. Once you figure out what's eating you up inside, you'll be the best the world has ever seen. I can sense it. One more thing."

Noa closed her eyes and asked, "Does the name Gabagool mean anything to you?"

Olivia laughed, "No, who's that?"

She opened her eyes and smiled, "I have no idea, but it has something to do with you, Jaxon and some man in a dark suit."

When she mentioned my name, I had to put a stop to this, "Alright, now that you're done cleansing her aura can I get to work on the physical side?"

"Sure honey." Before she walked away, she got closer to me and asked, "Do you trust me?"

"Of course, why?"

"Good because she's the one. Invest in her. Give her what she needs and she'll give it back to you tenfold. In a small sense, water her and watch her grow."

"I don't think she needs to grow anymore."

She chuckled, "Jaxon, give her what she needs, help her when you can, and your gratitude will come back to you tenfold. Trust me."

"Alright."

Noa said as she walked away. "Good luck out there."

Chapter 18

JAXON

Fifteen minutes after Noa left I had Josh get to work training on Olivia in the ring.

I watched as he explained to her a few basic moves to see what she could handle.

Then he walked away from her. He asked, "Ready?"

"Yep."

He tried to lunge after her. She put her arms out to stop him, but snuck under her arms and spun around to her back. Then he put his arms around her waist locking his fingers in place. He said, "This is what they call a wrestler's lock. Now try to undo my hands and get out of this."

She chuckled, "Are you kidding? You're barely holding me."

I saw him gritting his teeth and holding on tight, "Just try to."

Olivia used her strength, pulled his wrists, bent them back a little and then used her butt as a punching bag knocking Josh down fast.

I asked, "How's it going in there?"

Josh responded from the floor, "She's kicking my ass and we barely even started."

"Show her some…"

Before I could continue, my old client Heather Beckman came into the gym with her eleven-year-old daughter Becca, holding her mom's hand. Heather was in her early thirties. Long blonde hair and blue eyes. Very pretty. She always reminded me of an older Alexa Bliss. She retired from wrestling because of a bad injury.

Heather pulled my attention from Olivia, "Hey, Jaxon."

"Oh, hi Heather. Give me a second."

I yelled to Josh, "Show her a rope move and I'll be back in a few minutes."

Heather looked at Olivia and asked, "Who's the new girl?"

"Her name is Olivia."

"She's a…wow, she's a tall one."

"If I can train her right, she's going to be the next big thing in female wrestling."

"Big is an understatement."

My eyes glanced over at Becca for a second. She looked at Olivia with amazement. It almost looked like her eyes were about to pop out of her head.

I smiled and leaned over to Heather, getting closer to her ear, "She hates it when I tell people this, but I discovered her on the night of my bachelor party. She was oil wrestling at this hole in the ground gentleman's club. A literal hole-in-the-ground! It was an old bomb shelter or fallout shelter transformed into a strip bar."

"Seriously? A stripper?"

My hand blocked her from going any further, "Oh no! She made it very clear she never took her clothes off."

'Really?"

"She was the bouncer and she wrestled from time to time for extra money. This woman wasn't like any of the girls working there. She wore a one peace swimsuit; she didn't strip or do anything sexy and she had a demeaner in her eyes like she wanted to kill someone."

"Wow."

"All those other girls were touchy feely, not her. She kicked the crap out of the girl she fought. It was…frickin amazing. I knew she didn't belong there. So, I convinced her to be a professional wrestler."

Heather, her daughter, and I all watched as Josh bounced on the ropes, ran to Olivia, and hit her hard. Olivia moved a little, like a tall building swaying in the high wind, but it was generally like he ran into a wall. He slammed into her, but he fell down fast.

Heather smiled, "I assume it didn't take much convincing. She looks like a natural."

"I told you. There's something about her. That fire. That drive. She has it."

We all stood there for a moment watching Josh train her.

Then Heather told me, "Listen, I just came by to pick up some personal belongings. I moved out. I want everything in one place."

"I'm sorry to hear about you and Mike."

"It's alright. Becca and I are better off anyway."

"Okay, let's get your things. We can talk about that other stuff in the office."

Just as Olivia was taking a five-second break to wipe the sweat off her face, she saw Becca looking at her.

Becca still looked astonished by her size. Olivia smiled at the little girl then went back to training.

Chapter 19

OLIVIA

When I took a small break and got a drink of water, I noticed a little blonde girl walking around the gym. She looked to be ten maybe eleven. She had a sweet innocent look about her. She'd walk on a treadmill for a few seconds, get bored and head to a stepper. Getting closer and closer to the wrestling ring.

As she got closer to me as I trained her eyes snuck a peak at me. Her face gave off a very curious look. I thought it was odd that someone brought a little girl to a gym, but I smiled at her anyway. She was cute.

What was a little ten-year-old girl doing in a gym at 8 a.m. on a Monday? It only took me a second to realize, it was summer. Duh!

I took a breath and wiped the sweat off my face as Josh asked me, "Breaks over. Let's get back to it."

I put my water bottle to the side and responded, "Alright."

"Are you sure you never wrestled before? You seem to know a lot of these moves already."

I looked away for a second, trying to avoid the truth. I didn't want to tell him about The Rat Hole and the kind of wrestling they had there, "I did a little wrestling back in high school but there were no girl teams and guys didn't want to come near me. They were afraid of losing to a six-foot six girl. So, I just wrestled from time to time for fun."

"You catch on quick. You're a natural."

I smiled and nodded. "Thanks." Still trying to hide my actual wrestling experience at the bar.

"Just remember, no matter how good you are, and you are pretty good - you need to teach your body to take a hit and mostly not get hurt."

I threw my towel to the side as I said, "Jaxon told me he was more worried about me hurting them."

"He's right. With your size you can easily hurt someone badly if you don't know what you're doing. Wrestling is a show."

I shot him a look, "I don't want to come off fake though. Like a lot of the professional wrestlers, I see on TV are."

He gave me a small smile as he tilted his head in pride, "Ninety percent of all professional wrestling in America is fake or staged. If you don't want to look fake or be fake, then we have a lot of work to do."

"I don't. I want to be as real as I can be."

"Alright. I want to see how quick thinking you are."

I said with pride, "I'm ready for anything, Let's go."

Josh moved fast, raising his leg in the air, "If I kicked you in the stomach, like this..."

He put his foot out to try and kick me, but I grabbed his leg in mid-air. "Is this quick enough?"

He waved his arms out trying to maintain his balance as he said, "Fuck! Yep."

I let go of his leg so he could continue the training. He got his balance back and told me, "Alright, let's pretend I kicked you."

"But you didn't."

"I know, but let's say I did."

My smart-ass tongue whipped, "How about we pretend I took your foot I grabbed and twisted it, causing you to fall."

He didn't like that. His eyes narrowed, "Just follow me, will you."

"Fine."

"Now pretend you're in pain from the blow I made to your stomach area. I want you to bend down holding your stomach in pain."

I did what he asked by putting my hands on my stomach, as if he kicked me, keeled over, and did my best to 'pretend' to be in pain, "Ouch, my stomach hurts. Whatever shall I do?"

I looked up for a second with a smirk on my face. His face told me he didn't find it funny.

I chuckled, "You see, I have to be real because I'm terrible at acting. I can't do fake."

"I see. Moving on."

"Sorry. Okay, now what?"

"I'm going to attempt to do a move called The Sunset Flip. I need to see how fast you react to it, so I know what to show you next."

While I was bent over in — so called pain - Josh jumped over my back, but it was like a little person doing hurdles on a track. He managed to barely get over me and landed by my legs. With his next move he tried to use his arms to pull me down, but I let my body fall and sat on him. I'm sure it felt like a giraffe was parking its ass on his stomach.

He yelled in a little pain, "Oh shit!"

I quickly got off, "Oh, are you Okay?"

"Yeah, that was a quick-thinking defense move. Exceptionally good. Remember, if you would have landed too hard you could have really injured me badly. Good move, watch the landing though."

"Got it."

He took a deep breath and got back up on his feet then asked, "I weigh close to two thirty-five. Can you lift me?"

"I can lift my sister with ease so I can probably lift you too."

"I'm sure your sister weighs a lot less than me."

"True but I don't think it will be that hard to lift you, what do you want me to do?"

"I want you to try and body slam me on the mat. This is the most common move in wrestling, and I have a feeling you can do it with ease."

I twisted my lip and took a step back, "I just dropped my ass on your chest I thought you said to watch it so I don't hurt you."

He chuckled, "You're getting it now. Thanks for asking but I've been wrestling for close to twelve years. Training other wrestlers for three. I lost count on how many times I've been body slammed. You've banged me up a lot already. I'm sure I can take it."

"Aright, if you say so."

"Good, let's do it then."

Josh ran toward me. He put his hands on the upper part of my arm because he couldn't reach my shoulders. He tried to push me down using his feet, but I grabbed him, put my one arm around his head and my other arm in his groin area, and hoisted him up.

Two hundred and thirty-five pounds? He felt more like two hundred or one ninety. I did what he asked. I threw him on the ground and did the body slam.

He landed with a boom. At first, he didn't move.

I asked him, "Did I do it right?"

He moaned a response, "Yep. You did great."

"You're not hurt, are you?"

"Maybe a pinch."

"Need help up?"

He wheezed words out of his mouth, "Yes, please."

I held my hand out and helped him up.

He told me as he slowly got to his feet, "That's enough wrestling training for today."

I smiled a little, "Do you mean that's all you can take for now?"

"Yep, let's head to the weights. At least over there I won't get hurt."

I laughed, "Unless I drop a weight on your foot."

"Please don't."

As we left the wrestling ring to head to the weights, I saw him walking with a slight limp so I said, "You are hurt. I'm sorry."

"I've been through worse. I'll recover."

"Want me to carry you over there?"

He shot me a look. It clearly meant, no. That would damage his manhood.

Chapter 20

OLIVIA

Josh and I spent about twenty minutes in the wrestling ring for training and almost another thirty minutes lifting weights. This is where he kicked my ass.

The last thing Josh had me doing was arm curls with an easy bar. We did three sets. The first two sets were easy but he loaded the weight on for the third set. Thirty-five pounds on each side.

He counted as I did the last of my curls in my workout. "Twenty-three."

I could feel the veins in my neck about to pop as I strained, "Twenty-four…"

He shouted, "You can do it. Come on. One more."

"Twenty-five!" Then I dropped the bar on the floor, "Holy shit my arms hurt."

"You almost dropped that on my foot."

I laughed a little, "Oh, I'm sorry. It wasn't on purpose I swear."

Josh patted me on the back, "It's fine."

He was extremely impressed with me, "I'm amazed you got up to a seventy-pound easy curl. Most women tap out at forty or maybe fifty on the first day. No pain no gain, isn't that right baby?"

"Don't call me baby."

"Why not? It's just a pet name?"

I gave him a sarcastic look, "Because I'm not a pet. My name's Olivia. Not baby, honey, sweety, or anything like that."

He looked a little intimidated as he waved his hand toward me, "Okay, I get it. Sorry."

The workout made me sweat more than I ever have before. I took my towel and brushed all the wetness off my face. I assumed I looked like a hot mess.

Josh told me, "An hour workout and wrestling practice is pretty good for your first time."

"Thanks."

"Since it is your first day, let's skip tomorrow but come back on Wednesday for ninety minutes. This will give your body a day to recover."

I laughed, "And your body a chance to recover too?"

He gave me a stare, "Yes."

I took a drink of my water as he continued, "You will need to get your body used to doing this all the time though."

I guzzled down some water listening to him and responded, "Sounds good."

"Starting next week, I want you to start a regular routine workout schedule of six days a week."

I expelled a few deep breaths, "You're going to kill me."

"It's payback for today and all the days coming up where you're probably going to beat the crap out of me."

I gave him a stare and smiled, "I'll do my best but six days a week? Really?"

He took a drink and then finished with, "You wanted fast results. This is how it's done."

As I was walking toward the locker room, I heard him yell, "Don't forget to eat better and don't sit around. Do some walking and maybe some running. Keep your body moving."

"Got it."

This was the biggest and hardest workout I ever put myself through. The notion that I would have to put my body through this day in and day out to get better made me a little sick to my stomach.

However, my heart wanted this. I was in pain now, but I knew the pain would go away soon leading to remarkable results.

As I got out of the shower, I saw the same blonde-haired girl I noticed before when I was wrestling. She had a very pretty face and a nice smile. She was pulling some stuff out of a locker when I greeted her, "Hi."

"Hi. Olivia."

"How do you know who I am?"

"Jaxon told me. Plus, it's hard not to notice someone with your stature."

I laughed a little, "True. So, are you a wrestler too?"

She responded, "I was. I had a bad injury in the ring. I had to retire. I'm Heather by the way."

"Retire? You look young. Couldn't you heal and get back in there?"

Heather laughed a little as she said, "Thanks. I'm not that young. I'm thirty-one."

"Thirty-one? Are you kidding me? That's still young. Get yourself better and get back out there."

She smiled, "And spar with you, no thanks. My injury would just get worse."

I took off my towel and grabbed my underwear out of my locker.

Heather asked me, with an oddly shaky voice, "I'm at that age when most…ah, I…I'm sorry. Do, ah, do you want me to leave, while…ah, while you're getting dressed?"

"No, you don't have to. This is the women's locker room. We're both women."

"Okay, ah, anyway…it was hard to be a pro wrestler and take care of…of a…of a child too."

After pulling up my underwear I started to put on my bra, "Oh, that little girl I saw you with earlier. What's her name?"

Heather's voice evened out as she told me, "Her name is Becca. She ran off but I'm sure she's somewhere in here. She's been to this gym several times. She knows everyone and everyone here knows she belongs to me."

I put my old Bon Jovi concert t-shirt on and told her, "Yeah, I think most men are creeps, but Jaxon seems like a nice guy."

"He is. He took care of me when I wrestled. He sees wonderful things for you."

That comment made me smile.

She stared at me for a moment and said, "Your, ah…your shirt looks…"

"This old thing? Most clothes off the rack don't fit me. I have to shop in the big and tall men's section. Shirts like these are either too big or not long enough."

"No, that's not what I meant. I like Bon Jovi too."

That surprise me a little, "Oh."

Then Heather took a breath and asked me, "Hey, ah - you want to get some lunch? A post workout meal is particularly important. I should know."

I turned around to see Becca looking at me from behind a wall. I smiled and asked as I pointed to Becca, "Is she coming too?"

Becca then hid behind the wall. I smiled as I told her, "I don't bite."

Becca then quickly ran to her mom and hid behind her legs.

Heather brushed her fingers through Becca's hair and said, "Yea, she's kind of attached to me."

"Sure, I'm new to this healthy eating plan so you can give me a few pointers and tell me what to stay away from."

"Let's go to AJ's. It's a local place about two blocks from here."

"AJ's. I've been there a couple of times. Sure, sounds good. I'll meet you there in about twenty minutes."

Heather picked up her bag and out of the corner of my eye I saw Becca looking up at her mom, smiling.

Chapter 21

OLIVIA

When we met at AJ's, Heather ordered for me. Salmon, broccoli, a sweet potato, half of an avocado and an apple.

I smiled as I commented, "It looks, colorful."

Heather laughed a little, "I had to eat that way all the time when I wrestled. Boring but healthy."

I looked over at Becca's meal. A hot dog and fries. I told her, "Yours looks better."

Becca smiled.

Heather was eating chicken tenders and fries.

As I ate, I asked Heather, "When I left the gym Jaxon told me who you were, but he didn't tell me much about you except that you used to wrestle."

"Oh, well, my ex-husband is Mike 'The Mad Dog.' I met him when I was just nineteen. We got married right away and I had Becca when I turned twenty. We were a power couple in the wrestling world but we're getting a divorce now."

"Oh, I'm sorry to hear that."

"We were married for ten years but he became abusive in the last couple of years. That's another reason I want to retire. I didn't want my personal life to be brought up as banter in the ring."

Becca said with a monotone voice, "My dad was mean to us."

I brought food up to my mouth but stopped and sighed. This made me think of my mom and dad and how mean he was to me and my sister.

I confessed to Heather, "I know how it is. My dad, his name was also Mike, he was a drunk asshole."

As I swore, I looked over at Becca, "I'm sorry, I shouldn't have said that."

The girl said in an extremely sweet voice, "It's fine. I've heard worse when mom and dad were fighting."

I looked over at Heather, "Oh really."

Heather nodded, "We were both wrestlers so sometimes we had shouting matches."

"I'm sorry to hear that."

There was a moment of silence until I put my fork down and continued where I left off, "Here I am a six-foot six woman and I never tried to stop my dad from hitting my mom or my little sister. Until one day I had enough. I told him that I hated him, and I wished he was dead."

Heather was taken back, "Harsh words but it sounds like he deserved it."

"Maybe. I know. I regret it now. The day I said that he got really drunk and died in a car accident. I was only twenty."

Becca put her hand on my hand, "It wasn't your fault."

"I know but to this day, I wish I could take it back - wishing he was dead. I think I would have preferred him rotting in a jail cell."

Heather said, "Olivia, he sounds like he was a bad man. Very toxic."

"He was."

Becca added, "Wow, you have a lot in common with my mom."

I turned my head, "How so?"

"Both of you have had it rough." Becca then scooted her butt out of the booth.

"Where are you going, sweetie." Her mom asked.

"I have to go to the bathroom, mom."

"Do you want me to go with you?"

Becca shot her mom a look, "Mom, I'm eleven, not four. I'll be fine."

I told her, "If someone gives you any trouble just yell for me. I'll clobber them."

Becca smiled and told her mom, "I like her. She's a keeper."

When Becca left us, Heather's face got a little red as she said, "OOhh…kaayy. Kids. So unpredictable. Pay no attention to her."

"Why not? She's cute. No filter and brutal honesty. I like that. You know, I thought she was ten."

Heather watched me take a bite of my sweet potato and asked, "So, can I ask you something?"

"Sure."

She almost seemed nervous when she said, "Back at the gym you said you think all men are creeps. Why did you say that? Are you into girls?"

"I don't know. Nobody's ever asked me that before." As I sat there and pondered my past, I remembered I was never boy crazy. Maybe that's one of the reasons it never felt right with the boys I did date. Then again, back then, most boys were scared to death of me.

I took a bite of my salmon and continued, "Honestly, almost all the men I've ever talked to were assholes. My dad, my ex-boss Frank, and a few boys back in high school. Not to mention all the pervs at the bar where my sister works at. The only nice guy I've ever met was Jaxon. Get this, I originally thought he was a creep too. The first time he met me he poured oil on me."

Heather chuckled a little, "He told me you were an oil wrestler."

"He did, did he?", then I looked away feeling stupid, "Well, I guess I gave that info away for free when I said he poured oil on me. That was dumb of me."

"Shit. I'm sorry. He also told me you hated when people find out. I shouldn't have said anything."

"It's fine. I'm not mad. I was mostly the bouncer. My ex-boss Frank convinced me to wrestle. What an asshole he was."

I took another bite of sweet potato and continued, "Anyway, getting back to your question, I don't like labels. I understand that some people are proud to be whoever they are, but I don't want to be known as gay, bi or whatever. I want to like who I like without labels."

Heather smiled, "I like that."

"Like what?"

Then she looked at me in a strange way. "So, ah…are you going to Jaxon's wedding?"

"No, I wasn't invited."

"Do you want to go? You can be my plus one."

"Sure. It'll be fun. Oh, but I don't have a dress."

She smiled and said, "We could…" but she stopped when she saw Becca coming back from the bathroom at that moment.

I took another bite and asked Heather, "Are you okay?"

Heather told me, "Yeah, yea, I'm fine." Then she put her hand on her chin, took a deep breath and asked her daughter, "So…Becca. How was the bathroom?"

She answered with a sarcastic tone, "It's a bathroom mom. They're all the same."

As they were having a conversation about bathrooms, I got a text from my sister. "I'm sorry. I have to go. It's my sister."

Becca's lips pouted a little, "Leaving so soon?"

"Yeah, sorry. My sister and I only have one car, for now, and she wants me to take her somewhere. Heather, how much do I owe you for the lunch?"

Heather smiled and said, "Don't worry about it. Lunch is on me."

"You don't have to do that. We barely know each other."

"It's fine. I liked getting to know you better over lunch. Seriously, my treat."

"Alright then, thanks."

As I scooted out of my seat I asked, "Will you be coming back to the gym again sometime?"

With a small sparkle in her eye she smiled, "Definitely."

"Good. I'll see you around then."

As I walked to the door I saw out of the corner of my eye, Becca gave her mom a napkin.

Heather asked her, "What's this for?"

Becca told her mom, "Your drool."

Heather threw it back to her.

That made me laugh as I walked out.

Chapter 22

OLIVIA

When I walked into my apartment, I quickly noticed the smell of a few scented candles burning. Was she trying to mask the smell of something she smoked? It didn't matter. As long as the place didn't smell like funk and sex like it did the other night.

Emma was watching TV drinking a beer. I asked, "You're drinking before noon? I thought I had to take you somewhere?"

"Oh, you did but I took care of it. Sorry, I forgot to hit you back."

I expressed my frustration in her, "You know, you're only nineteen. If you ever get caught drinking, they might put you in jail. It's bad enough our mom is in prison."

She said with a smug smile, "Na, never gonna happen. I have a fake ID thanks to Frank, remember?"

This is what really frustrates me about my sister. She put all her faith in that con man Frank. Plus, when she needs me, she expects me to come running. I'm sure she's grateful for my help but she's not very polite when it comes to others, "Emma, I was having lunch with…oh never mind. I'm here now."

She asked, "How was training today?"

"My arms are killing me. First day of training in the ring was easy but the weightlifting was hard."

"Weightlifting?"

"Jaxon wants me to bulk up."

"Does he want you to be a sumo wrestler?"

I laughed, "No, he wants me to add more muscle."

"Oh, that makes sense."

I went to get a drink of water from the refrigerator and saw a new drawing of a beautiful flower hanging on the door like a little kid's masterpiece. "Emma, did you draw this?"

"Yeah, I don't like it though. You can have it if you want it."

I smiled as I opened the door thinking about how talented she is.

The smile faded quickly, and my frustration grew when all I saw was beer, "Where's the bottled water?"

"Oh, I'm sorry. I used the last bottle this morning to make coffee after you left for the gym."

Again, this would have been useful information to know as I rushed over.

"So, there's no water, anywhere in this place?"

"Sure, there is. Do like we did when we were kids. Get a glass from the cabinet and get water from the sink."

She knew I bought bottled water because the sink water here tasted really bad. I'm sure that's why she used the bottled water for her coffee.

After looking at all the alcohol in the fridge and the empty cans in the garbage I made a difficult decision without delay. I needed to move out. I love my sister but being around her and worrying about how she lives her life is something I couldn't deal with anymore.

I sat down across from Emma and told her, "Listen, I want to move out on my own but like I told you before, I'm worried about you."

As she took a sip of beer she asked, "What do you mean?"

I stated the hard facts, "Who will keep an eye on you? Someone has to make sure you don't go down a dark path."

"Dark path? I like having my 'big sister' to look after me at the club but it's about time you moved out and made a life for yourself."

I was surprised that came out of her mouth, "Wait, you want me to move out?"

She swallowed down another gulp of her drink and said, "Yes. My sister is going to be a professional wrestler. You don't need me and my friends to keep you up at night."

She took another drink of her beer and continued, "Besides, I can't wait to see you beat the crap out of someone. Every time you wrestled at the bar you were a sight to see. You never lost."

I could almost feel my cheeks start to get red, "Oh God. Don't remind me about that. I hate that people are going to ask me, '*So Olivia, how did you get your start?*' and I have to respond, '*Some guy saw me oil wrestling.*' That's so embarrassing."

Emma got up and strolled to the fridge. Her stride had a little bit of a wobble to it, "Why? Everyone starts somewhere and unlike all the other girls there, me included, you never took your clothes off."

I began to think she might have a point, "I suppose you're right but still, if I make it big, is 'oil wrestler' good to put on a professional wrestler's resume?"

She moved slowly in a nearly robotic fashion as she returned from her trip to the kitchen and popped open another beer. She sat and said, "I see what you mean but you could also inspire people too."

I smiled and said thick with sarcasm, "Yeah, right. I can see the caption now, 'Were you a sexy oil or mud wrestler? Well, clean yourself up and dream big because you can be a professional wrestler just like Olivia."

We both laughed.

Emma's eyes were starting to look glassy and unfocused but even in this state she was in she said something that really made me think, "You do realize that of all the nights to come to the Rat Hole that guy came on a night you were there, wrestling. Not a night when you were a ref. Not a night when you were a bouncer. He's a sports promoter who had his bachelor party on a night when you were wrestling."

I nodded my head, "Strange, Jaxon said that same thing to me the night we talked. I suppose you're right."

"I know I'm right. Now look at you. Training to be a professional wrestler."

I smiled at her. Despite all the crazy shit that Emma does I don't think I'll ever forget this conversation. My little sister told me this was meant to be.

She said, "Seriously, this is a golden opportunity for you."

Then I stood up as I told her, "Since you don't need me here now, I'm going to go look at this apartment I saw when I drove here."

"Okay. Oh, before I forget, Becky is getting rid of her car."

I raised my eye brows, "I don't know if I want to buy a car from someone I beat up."

"Not for you, for me. You can have my car and I'll buy hers."

"That would work. I like your car. It's small for me but it will due for now until I can afford to get me another truck."

As I grabbed the door knob, I told her with sincerity, "I'll always be here if you need me."

"I know."

When I opened the door to walk out, I heard the bathroom door open so I turned my head for a second. Walking out of the bathroom was the bald dude with the snake tattoo. He was surprised to see me, "Olivia? What are you doing here?"

"I live here. Emma is my sister."

"No fucking way! Emma told me you were The Queen Bee, but I never put it together that you two were related."

"Yes way, but I'll be moving out soon."

Emma got up and hugged him, "Olivia this is Tim. Tim, this is my sister Olivia."

Tim smiled, "We met in the hallway a few days ago didn't we baby?"

My whole body tensed up as I crossed my arms, "I'm not your baby."

"I call all women 'baby.'" Then he looked at Emma, "Isn't that right baby?"

Just before Emma kissed him on the lips she said, "That's right."

My nostrils flared, "You can call her baby but not me, got it?"

He seemed a little annoyed that I didn't allow him to call me what he wanted, "Whatever."

I could feel the heat fuming on my head as I was getting increasingly angry at this guy because I know he was with my sister, "Yet another reason I'm moving out."

As I was just about to close the door I told Emma, "If this asshole gives you any trouble, you know how to get a hold of me."

"Trouble? What trouble?"

My sister is sometimes as blind as a bat.

Chapter 23

JAXON

On Wednesday morning, as I opened the gym, I got a text from Heather at 8 a.m.

Are you busy?

Can I come to the gym and talk to you?

That was an odd request. Very early for her too. I responded.

Eric is back. I opened. He's taking care of the rest.

I have meeting today at Westman's.

I'll be at the gym on Friday.

Can we talk on Friday?

Sure. Does Fri at 10am sound good?

Sounds great. See you Friday.

I had no idea what she was up to. I thought she wanted all her stuff in one place? She's retired from wrestling and also injured. Why does she need to come to a gym?

When Friday came, as I walked around the gym, I saw Heather stroll in at 9am. That was super early for our meeting. She almost looked lost until she found what she was looking for. She started watching Olivia train.

For a few seconds, I watched what she was looking at. Olivia took Josh's arm, twisted it in back of him and then flipped him over slamming him on the mat.

My head turned to Heather just in time to see her flinch when Josh hit the floor.

Heather looked like she gasped as she put her hand over her mouth to keep from saying something.

She was so occupied watching Olivia I snuck up behind her and said, "She's amazing…"

My voice nearly gave her a heart attack. She screamed and jumped back, "Ahh, what the…?"

I couldn't help but laugh. "I'm sorry. Did I scare you?"

She smacked my arm, "No…I was…I…" Then she turned her head away from me, so I couldn't see her red cheeks. She finally answered, "I was getting myself familiar with the place."

I raised one eyebrow toward her, "Really? You've worked out here hundreds of times over the course of two years. It hasn't changed."

She couldn't think of a new answer, "Well, I…ah…I wanted to be…on time so…"

"You're an hour early for our meeting."

She sighed then confessed, "Alright fine. Truth is, since I'm not wrestling anymore, I need a job."

I saw her look down, almost as if she was ashamed to ask me. She slowly lifted her head again but her eyes gravitated toward the wrestling ring as I asked, "Really? You're a former professional wrestler. I'm sure…"

I didn't get a chance to finish.

Noa walked next to us. It was as if she heard and saw our whole conversation. She told Heather, "I need a person to clean the gym Monday, Wednesday and Friday, after we close down for the night. My current cleaning person isn't doing a very good job."

I told Noa, "Don't you think going from professional wrestler to janitor is a step down?"

Noa saw Heather looking at Olivia again, "I'll pay you twenty dollars an hour. You can work out and use the gym anytime you want. Take as long as you need to do the job just make sure it doesn't smell like a high school boys…"

Without skipping a beat Heather agreed, "I'll take it."

I had to ask again, "Heather, are you sure? I mean…"

Noa grabbed my face and turned it toward the wrestling ring. All three of us watched as Olivia knocked Josh down, landed on top of him and grabbed his leg for a pin.

Noa said, "She's sure."

Chapter 24

HEATHER

A few hours later, after Olivia and I had lunch again, I returned to my apartment in a cheerful and perky mood. The smile on my face could not be ignored.

Becca was watching TV as she saw me come in. She asked, "Why are you so happy? It looks like someone put a hanger in your mouth."

I could feel the heat in my cheeks start to ignite as I looked away. I took a breath and told her, "For your information, we're not going to starve. I got a job."

"Eating is good. It must be a really good job to make you this happy?"

I sat down next to her and said, "Noa gave me a job at the gym."

"Doing what?"

"Cleaning the gym."

Becca put out her tongue and shook her head as she flipped through some channels, "Disgusting. That place sometimes reeks of funky sweat. Now you're going to clean it?"

I got up and went to my bedroom to get changed as I answered, "Yes. I start today. Well, tonight."

Becca asked, "Are we hurting for money? I thought you got some residuals when cable channels do reruns of your old matches."

"The residuals don't pay squat and we're not hurting, yet. I have a good savings but it's not going to last forever."

"Whatever mom. I think you should use your wrestling experience. Coaching, training, managing, something besides cleaning a gym but it's your…"

I found it very odd that she didn't finish her sentence so I looked out from my room and saw what stopped her. She was watching a rerun of my old wrestling matches.

I walked out slowly.

She asked, "You miss wrestling, don't you?"

I slowly walked out in my bra and jeans because I didn't know what to say, "Kinda, maybe. Actually, no. Not really. I'm retired."

As I walked away, I added, "You know, Noa said I can use the gym anytime I want now. Want to come workout a little tomorrow. Let's say 10 a.m.?"

"Ten in the morning? On a Saturday?"

"Yeah, like we used too?"

I walked out from the bedroom with my old jeans and t-shirt on, ready for a night of cleaning. Becca looked at me with a strange stare. I asked, "What? Do I look bad?"

She wondered, "Will Olivia be there tomorrow?"

My daughter is too smart for her own good.

"I think so, why?"

"I'll pass. I don't like to watch her sweat as much as you do."

"What…no. That's not why I got the job."

She smiled a mischievous grin at me, "Who said anything about the job. I was talking about tomorrow."

"Well, I mean…we need money and…"

"Sure mom, whatever."

I took the small pillow off the couch and threw it at her just before I walked out the door.

Chapter 25

OLIVIA

A few weeks went by, and my sister helped me move into my new apartment. It was an extremely balmy day in August. Over ninety degrees out. Luckily moving in was easy for me since I didn't have much stuff to move.

We pulled into the complex. It was a dirty ground level apartment building. The fence dividing each apartment had many vines growing on it hiding the desperately needed paint job. The whole place was run down and disordered. It looked cheap.

Emma had to state her opinion, "Fernwoods Apartments?" Then she looked at me with concern.

"What? It was all I could afford for now."

As we pulled up to the front door, she sipped her drink and then she told me, "Sis, I love how you're moving out and giving me more privacy, but this place is a dump."

"Hey, it was five hundred and fifty dollars a month."

She changed her tune, "Not bad. A lot better than what I'm paying."

When I opened the car door, the cool air from the air conditioning escaped fast like an air lock on a spaceship. The ninety-two-degree humidity hit us fast.

Waves of heat rose off the pavement like flames on a roof. As we walked up to my new apartment I told her, "With your job you can afford what you're paying. I can't anymore."

"What do you mean? You made a killing when you were wrestling at the Rat Hole, and you hardly spent any of it."

I walked into my new home and showed her the place. I cranked up my air and said, "I know, but now I am. At one time I had over twelve thousand dollars in my savings but now it's depleting fast. I only get paid when I wrestle, and I haven't wrestled in a single match yet."

The whole place was one spacious room except for the kitchen and bathroom. The kitchen was small, and the bathroom was even smaller.

When Emma looked around, she smiled, "It's actually not that bad. Pitiful, bare, and empty but also tiny, cute, and cozy. It's small so it should cool off quick."

"I know. Thanks."

I sighed and looked at her, "You know, this place reminds me of the apartment mom and dad had just before they got married. That was a one bedroom but this is smaller."

"I don't remember."

"You wouldn't. You were just a baby. We didn't move into the new place until you were three." I took a quick drink of water and added, "It used to drive dad nuts when you hid in the closet and played with your dolls alone. He wanted you to go outside."

"Yea, I vaguely remember that. Maybe I hated people."

We both walked out to my car to get boxes full of my stuff. Rivets of sweat poured off of us from the summer heat blaring down as we worked.

Emma asked, "Where's your bed going?"

I gave her a disappointed look, "I'm not going back for it."

"You have to sleep on the floor? Olivia, this place is made for a dwarf not someone your size. When you lie down, your toes and head will hit the walls."

I told her with a deep sarcastic tone, "Funny."

I put my boxes down on the floor and continued, "Very few beds fit me, remember. It was bad enough my feet hung off the edge of my bed at your apartment."

"Mom and dad had that bed for twenty years."

"It's about time we junked it."

It felt like we were walking into an oven as we walked out to my car to get more boxes, "I was going to visit mom this weekend but I ended up moving out instead."

"We're both busy. I'm sure she understands."

"You know, you should visit mom."

She ignored me, "Olivia. Let me buy you a new bed."

"Thanks, but where would I put it? This place is like a shoe box."

She smiled with a hit of sarcasm, "Next to the shoestrings."

"I'll be fine. Let's visit mom this weekend. She really wants to see you."

We walked into my cool small room that I now call a living space and set the boxes down.

Again, she ignored what I said, "Looks like this is your last box. Is that all the help you need? My cup's empty and I got a text from…"

"Emma. Our mom is in prison, and she wants to see you!"

Emma screamed at me, "Well, maybe I don't want to see her, alright!"

"Why not?"

She shook her head and looked away ashamed, "I saw her in that place once. I hated it. Prison is awful. I don't ever want to go back there again."

"Is that really the reason?"

She let out a nervous breath still not facing me, "Yes."

"I'll go with you. Hell, I'll even hold your hand if I…"

Her voice cracked as she walked out of my apartment, "I don't want to go back there because I might end up like her, alright?"

"Emma, you won't end up like her. You have an incredible artistic talent. Leave the Rat Hole. Go to art school and…"

I assume she was tired of listening to me because she abruptly walked away.

Emma swiftly left my new home and stood by my car. The extreme heat didn't seem to bother her now as she wanted me to give her a ride back to her place.

Now that I was living on my own, I knew I wouldn't be able to keep an eye on her all the time like I was.

My gut told me that she might end up in the same place as our mom or worse.

Chapter 26

OLIVIA

After I moved out, I put all my focus on training. I was living on my own now, I had a car and I was focused on being the best wrestler I could be. I was also eating healthier than I have in my life and my body felt better because of it.

Occasionally Heather would pop in the gym. I saw her biking or walking on the treadmill a few times. Never any weights. We also went out to lunch a few times too. Sometimes Becca was with her and other times she wasn't.

Sadly, since I was so driven to get my body in shape, I didn't visit my mom in prison as much as I should have. I didn't forget about her. I was motivated to be a professional wrestler and I had a goal to achieve.

Within six weeks of the start of my training, I felt like a whole new person.

Jaxon thought it was going to take two to four months for me to get my body where it needed to be, but I was progressing very quickly. I put in the effort and worked hard six days a week, ate the right food to get my body in shape and put on fifteen pounds of muscle. My body was looking more tone and defined.

As I was leaving the locker room, about to head out the door and go home, Jaxon pulled me into the office, "Before you go, come here. I want to talk to you."

As we walked into the office again, I asked, "Is this your office today or that other guys?"

"You mean, Noa's brother Eric?"

"Yeah, I've never seen him."

"He's in Baltimore this weekend for a conference. I'm helping Noa out again. I'm sure you'll see him sometime."

"If he's real."

Jaxon gave me a droll smile as he sat down.

"I'm kidding."

"Anyway, I see you developed your skills and got your body in shape a lot quicker than I thought. Do you think you're ready to try a wrestling match?"

I smiled and got a little excited, "Yeah. Sure. When? What league?"

"This weekend and I'm sorry, it's not a league yet. This will be an exceedingly small underground match. A company is putting on a show for college students in Fort Wayne, Indiana."

I questioned, "It's a college match?"

"No, it's for college kids. The club is called IPWL. Indiana Pro Wrestling League. They'll be about six matches all together. The first few are on the wrestling team for the college, but the last two matches are like you, up and coming pro wrestlers."

"The pay can't be good."

"You're right. Only a hundred dollars. After taxes and our cut, it won't be much, but this will be your first paid wrestling show."

I took a deep breath and told him, "Listen, Jaxon, I love working out here. I've come so far, and I don't want to give up but I'm living off my savings. It's depleting fast. I'm going to need a part-time job like really soon to pay for food and other things."

I saw him turn his head and think. Then he looked at a picture of Noa on his desk. He said, "A few weeks before we met Noa told me I might meet that one big client that will change everything for me. She was right, I met you."

"Yeah, bachelor party, the stars aligned or something. You talked about that before."

"I'm getting there. Your first day of training. Noa told me to help you. Water you and watch you grow because someday you'll be huge, and my help will pay off."

I smiled, "Water me? Am I a tree?"

He laughed, "You're as tall as a tree. Anyway, what I'm trying to say is, don't worry about a part-time job. Your job is to train every day to be the best female wrestler on the planet. My job is to find you wrestling matches so we both get paid. If you need money for anything, just ask."

That was sweet of him but I shook my head, "No, I can't do that."

He put the picture down and sat up straight, looked me in the eye and said, "Olivia, I believe in you. I know you're going to be the best wrestler the world has ever seen. In just six weeks you turned your body into a tough machine. Six weeks! It usually takes girls four to six months. You put in the work and showed me how much you really want this. I trust you won't take advantage of me and this fantastic opportunity that's placed in front of you. So, I say again, if you need money, just ask. Okay?"

Nobody has ever put that much trust in me before. I responded with a few tears welling up in my eyes, "Okay."

"Now that we got the finances out of the way, if you do well this weekend, I'll have another match for you next weekend which will pay more and then we'll break for the weekend of my wedding."

I smiled at him and asked, "Two weeks until the big day. Is everything ready for the walk down the aisle?"

"Mostly. Thanks for asking. Oh, that reminds me, I need to give you an invitation."

I smiled and told him, "That's not necessary."

"Oh, of course it is. You're going to be the biggest wrestler on…"

I laughed a little, "No, what I'm saying is Heather invited me. I'm her plus one."

Jaxon had a delightful smile on his face. As if he was very happy to hear I was going with her, "That's wonderful."

Then he shook his hands and got back on track, "Anyway, let's stay focused. In Saturday's match you'll come out as the last match of the night because most people won't expect you, the six-foot six powerhouse."

That same thinking almost sounded like when Frank had me be the last wrestler of the night at the strip club. God, his words still echo in my brain. *'Guys will love to see you, the super tall girl, beating up on someone small.'* I can't wait to rub my professional wrestling career in his face.

I asked Jaxon, "Will I always be the last match?"

"I don't know. If you are, that's a good thing. The last match is the headliner. The Main Attraction. The crowd will always stay if you give them the best show last."

I finally understood the marketing behind me always being last. Keep the audience waiting. I told him, "Sounds great."

I got up to go home but he wasn't done. He said, "Oh, and one more thing before you leave, for now, you're still The Queen Bee."

I was greatly disappointed, "Oh come on. Really?"

"Yes, if you want the gig, you'll have to be The Queen Bee at least one more time. We'll have a meeting in my office at Westman's to discuss a better name later. You can change the suit a little, if you hate it that much but for now…you're still the Queen Bee."

I walked out slightly irritated, "Fine."

The thought of me wearing a black and yellow striped onesie, like my bathing suit, made me want to vomit. I needed to change my outfit quick.

Chapter 27

OLIVIA

A few days later, on a Saturday night, I was ready to do my very first professional wrestling match.

Jaxon was right. This first match was in a ridiculously small place. It almost looked like an old high school gymnasium, but he assured me, it was a college.

They had five different matches before me. The college kids did their wrestling thing first. Then the match right before me were two up-and-coming professional female wrestlers from a wrestling school in Ohio. Their names were Patrisha and Gina.

From behind the curtain, I watched as these two wrestlers put on a good show for the crowd. Is this what they wanted? A show?"

As their match was going on my challenger came up to me, "Hi Olivia."

I turned around and immediately recognized her, "Crystle?"

She wore a two-piece black and green outfit that looked exceptionally good on her. She smiled and said, "My wrestling show name is Lexy now but yeah, it's me. I see you still have some yellow in your outfit. Are you still the Queen Bee?"

I smiled, "Unfortunately yes. I'm going to change it after tonight, I hope. These colors remind me of those days at the fucking bar."

"You're tall. Use something with your height."

I laughed, "Of course."

We both watched Patrisha and Gina wrestle through a small crack in the curtain. My eyes widened as I saw Patrisha put Gina in a Camel Clutch as she let out a painful scream.

Crystle asked, "So, I take it you're not working for Frank anymore."

"Oh my God no. I can't stand him."

She asked me, "I'm glad you quit there too. Did Frank ever try and con you into sucking his dick?"

"No. If you remember; I told him I was never going to be naked in that place. That also meant no BJ's either. I wasn't a baby gravy dumpster like those other girls."

We both looked out as we heard a loud boom from the ring.

I continued, "Unfortunately, that rule didn't seem to stick with him. He paid Becky to try and rip my clothes off when we oil wrestled, so I beat the living shit out of her in the ring and then beat him up too. Then I quit."

She smiled, "I wish I would have been there to see that. His walk of shame was real. I wasn't about to fall for his crap. That's why I quit that night. Frank was an ass."

"I know. Sadly, I didn't find out until later when I broke the door down on his office after I beat the shit out of Becky."

She laughed.

I pointed to the ring, "Looks like we're up. Want me to go easy on you?"

"No, I mud wrestled you already. This can't be any worse."

I shot her a look, "Are you sure?"

"Yeah, I'm sure. If I'm going to be a professional wrestler, I have to train myself to take the hits, even from someone your size."

I snickered, "Okay, if you say so."

Then it was time for us. The announcer told everyone, "The last match of the evening are two wrestlers making their professional wrestling debut. The first one stands five foot seven. Weighing in at one hundred and ninety-two pounds, It's Lexy the Lock."

She walked to the ring, waving and smiling to everyone. The people were welcoming to her. They cheered and clapped a little.

He continued, "Next, also making her professional wrestling debut is her challenger. Standing six feet six inches tall weighing two hundred and fifteen pounds it's - The Queen Bee!"

When he said that name, I turned my head and flipped my tongue out. It made me sick but I had to deal with it for now.

They opened the curtain. When I walked out the crowd went nuts when they saw me. I was dressed in a black body suit with a bright yellow vertical stripe down each side. Similar to my yellow bathing suit when I wrestled at The Rat

Hole, but different. This was more of a body suit. Less horizontal stripes.

Lexy's eyes opened up as wide as saucers when she saw me. I laughed when I saw her shake her head and yell, "Nope!" She just did that for show. It's the same reaction she expressed when we mud wrestled.

I overheard her manager telling her that if she wrestled me tonight, she'll be the first one to fight me in my wrestling career. Win or lose, she'll be the first.

We already wrestled once before but I assume she didn't tell the person she was with about our mud match.

I looked over to all the people watching us and I saw a few people taking pictures and some even recording video. Or where they live-streaming? I couldn't tell for sure. One thing was certain, a lot of cameras were on this small-time match.

The bell rang three times – DING, DING, DING! It was time to get started.

As the match began, I did what she requested. I did not go easy on her. She was small but I knew what she was and wasn't capable of.

Lexy ran after me and grabbed my sides as if she was a linebacker in a football game. I quickly grabbed her head, locked it under my arm, grabbed her body, lifted her up and then threw her on the mat, backwards. This popular slam move is called the Fallaway Slam.

She hit the ground with a thud. Not hurt yet, she shook off her fall then tried to grab my legs to pull me down. I bent down and pulled her body up again, like she was a rag doll, and then threw her down hard for the second time. This time she hit the mat so hard, the sound echoed in the room. She screamed, "Oh crap!"

I hope I didn't hurt her, but Jaxon did say, he was more worried about me hurting someone else than other people hurting me.

I assume this audience wanted a show, so I gave them what they wanted. I jumped up and dropped my leg on her stomach. She screamed again, "Ahhh!"

The crowd went nuts screaming and cheering. The drunk pervs at the strip bar were loud, but these people were different. The feeling I got from them was general enthusiasm not horny men wanting to see my boobs.

We were only thirty seconds into our match and poor Lexy was breathing heavy lying flat on the ground, holding her stomach.

She tried to sit up and get away, but I turned her over on her stomach and locked my hands under her neck then pulled. This was the same move I saw Patrisha put Gina in a few minutes ago. It's also the oldest hold in wrestling. The Camel Clutch.

I only drew on her neck for a few seconds, just to give the audience something to be thrilled about. Seeing someone in pain. For a small venue this place was roaring with excitement.

My hands could almost feel the pressure of her veins in her neck as I kept pulling her head up. Her jaw clenched and her arms stiffened as she tried to move but couldn't.

Her hand raised like she was going to tap out. I didn't want to win that way, so I let her go. I wanted to win by a pin, like I did before.

Standing up, I looked at her and watched as she turned herself over. Gasping for air, her chest was going up and down faster than a frog's vocal sac.

It reminded me of the day we mud wrestled. She is not made for wrestling, mud or professional. I could see the expression in her face. It meant, let this be over. She was done.

I lowered myself to her body, grabbed her leg, raised it as high as it could go to make sure her shoulders were locked on the mat and pinned her in under a minute. As I raised her leg, I leaned my head down to her face and said, "Just like the old days?"

Trying to breathe, she told me through the gritting of her teeth, "Yep. Same as before. Still hurts. Only less messy."

The audience counted, "One… two… three!"

It was over!

I had won my first professional wrestling match. This felt so different than when I wrestled at the Rat Hole. I felt a feeling of joy rush over me.

I helped her up and asked Lexy, "Crystle, are you alright? I didn't hurt you, did I?"

She cracked a smile, "It's Lexy, remember?"

"Oh shit. That's right. Sorry."

"It's alright. It hurts worse than before. The mat was a lot softer back then."

We were about to leave the ring when she said, "I have to go ice my whole body."

"I'm glad my first professional wrestling match was you."

She laughed, "First one to mud wrestle you and now this."

I put my finger over my lips, "Shhhh! Let's not talk about that place, Lexy."

"Okay."

She walked away and I asked, "Hey, remember a long time ago when you said this isn't for me."

She smiled, "Yea, I remember."

"Were you talking about the bar or wrestling."

"The bar but after what we did just now, I think that implies to wrestling too. Take care Olivia."

"You, too."

As I walked out of the ring Jaxon asked me, "That was quick. Do you know her?"

"She was the first person I wrestled at The Rat Hole. It's strange that she's the first person I wrestled in my professional wrestling career too."

"Noa would say there are no strange coincidences."

We both said at the same time, "Everything happens for a reason." Then we both laughed.

I asked him, "How did I do for my first time?"

"Great."

"Was it over too quick? Should I have drawn it out more? Played with her a little, do more moves on her?"

He laughed, "No, you did fantastic."

"I didn't want to hurt her, but the crowd seemed to love the 'show' so I…"

He pointed to everyone in the audience, "You came out strong with a Fallaway Slam. No, you did two body slams, a Camel Clutch and you won in under a minute. They seemed to like it."

I got out of the ring and smiled. "Thanks." Then I turned around and watched Crystle walk away limping. I hope I didn't hurt her too bad.

Jaxon tapped me on the side, "Someone else is excited too."

Heather walked up to us. She was wearing a long black dress with very small yellow dots splashed all over it. The dress and yellow color made her blonde hair shine. She looked very nice. Smiling she said, "Congratulations on your first win."

"Thanks."

"Did Jaxon tell you? I lost my first match in this very same place."

"No, he didn't tell me that."

Jaxon said to Heather, "You turned out pretty well though."

"I'm so happy for you, Olivia."

I asked her, "So where's the little one?"

"She's spending some time with my mom." Then she gave Jaxon a look.

I told Jaxon, "I think I should hit the showers before we go home."

Heather chuckled and asked, "What for? You hardly broke a sweat."

Jaxon laughed. "She's right."

Then she asked, "Can I take you two out to celebrate?"

Jaxon looked at Heather. His eyes scoped out her dress then he twisted his lips as if he was thinking about something. They stared at each other for a moment then he told us, "Sorry, I have to go home to my woman but why don't you two go out."

"Sure. Let me get cleaned up first, okay Heather?"

I saw Jaxon lean over and tell Heather something, but I had no idea what it was.

Chapter 28

HEATHER

A few hours later, as Olivia and I sat down eating dinner, I admired her as she ate. She wore blue jeans and a simple all black t-shirt. Her brown wavy hair was rich and deep. Each strand tumbled, reflecting the rays of the sunset through the window. She seemed very happy.

Olivia took a bite of her steak and asked, "What did Jaxon whisper to you?"

I was a little embarrassed as I confessed, "He didn't really have to go home to Noa. He wanted us to hang out."

Olivia took another bite and beamed me a satisfying smile as I continued, "I love my daughter more than anything in the world, but I rarely get a chance to go out, alone, or with anyone."

Olivia seemed a little surprised. "Oh, so, Heather. Is this…a date then?"

I almost choked at her question, "This is me taking my friend out to celebrate her first win as a professional wrestler." I paused and then continued, "Unless you want to call it a date?"

She smiled back at me, "This does seem different then when we had lunch at AJ's a few times without Becca. We can call - *this* - a date."

My happiness reflected back at her as we enjoyed the moment.

As the night went on, we talked about all sorts of stuff. Movies, TV shows, and of course, wrestling too. Somehow, we got on the subject of me, and my ex-husband.

I ended up talking about him for a little while. "I got married at a young age. He was a good father to Becca, in the beginning. Mike and I had a great relationship for the first few years. We were the 'it' couple in the wrestling world."

Olivia ate a slice of an apple, drank some water, as she continued to listen. She was a particularly good listener even though I think I told her some of this before. She didn't seem to mind.

I continued, "Back then the sex was good to. We experimented with some light bondage from time to time but after a while he got too rough and took it too far."

Then I laughed.

She asked, "What's so funny?"

"I just remembered. One time we got a pool and had sex in lots of baby oil."

Olivia smiled, "Baby oil is better than vegetable oil. Trust me, I know from experience."

I laughed too but then sighed. "I'm sorry. I shouldn't be talking about sex with my ex-husband."

"It's okay. The light bondage sounds interesting but I...I..." She stopped as if she said something she shouldn't have.

I was surprised she said something about the light bondage. I gave her a shy smile back but then I questioned, "But what?"

She turned her face away from me as if she was trying to hide, "It's…it's nothing."

Suddenly it hit me, "Wait, are you still a virgin?"

She took a deep breath, blushing a little and confessed, "Yes."

I was a little shocked. "You're kidding? That was just a stupid guess. I thought you said you know from experience?"

Olivia lowered her head trying not to face me, "Well, you guessed right and 'experience' was about oil wrestling in baby oil, not sex."

I looked at Olivia, remembering back to her amazing win in the wrestling ring just a few hours ago, and my mind bubbled with curiosity. I responded with, "Oh, I see. I just assumed with your…stature, you – well, you know."

She took a breath and finally faced me again, "Oh, there were plenty of opportunities, but all guys wanted was a big girl to sit on them or step on them. I wasn't into that. I don't like being treated like a sex object."

At that moment, I felt happy to be talking to her, "I'm very proud of you."

She didn't say anything at first. The growing smile on her face said it all.

I took a sip of my drink and admired her again. There was a small moment of peaceful silence between us.

Unexpectedly she asked, "So if we were to ever, ah…you know."

I almost spit out my drink, "Oh boy! That's forward."

"I'm just sayin, you know. If we did. Would I still be a virgin?"

I laughed, "First off, I grew up Catholic. I was taught that a girl is no longer a virgin if she had sex with a man. I left that life behind – and that way of thinking - when I got married."

I took a drink of water and continued, "Next, I slowly realized that virginity is a man-made construct. If a woman breaks her hymen on a bicycle, is she still a virgin or did she actually have sex with a bike?"

Olivia couldn't help but laugh at that remark. "I only ask because you're the first person that didn't want me to step on them, or sit on them, or beat them up."

"I get it."

Her voice nervously cut off a few times as she continued, "You're the first person I met, next to Jaxon, who didn't want to use me. You talked to me. We're friends. Maybe even…I don't know. So, I thought, you know. If that ever happened."

I raised my hand. "I'm going to stop you right there. When and if we ever do anything in bed, I'll make sure it's special for you because of the information you shared with me."

"Thank you."

"Like I said, Jaxon thinks the world of you and…well, I like you too."

"Same. But please, no labels."

"You can be you. Pro wrestler. The amazing Queen Bee."

Olivia smiled with a hint of embarrassment, "Yeah, about that name. Jaxon and I are going to try and find a better one. That was my show name when I wrestled at that hole in the ground bar, and I want to leave that life behind."

"Then why did Jaxon want you to use it tonight?"

"I don't know. He said something about brainstorming and coming up with a better name later but we had to use The Queen Bee tonight."

I snickered, "Sounds like this match was a last-minute booking and he wasn't prepared to give you a new name yet."

"I hope so. I always hated that name. The Queen Bee. Bees are tiny. I'm not…"

I laughed and let out a sigh of relief, "Oh thank God. I hated that name too. The yellow on you is not very flattering."

"Why didn't you tell me?"

"I didn't want to hurt your feelings. I didn't know if you liked that name because it was from your grandma or whatever. I bought this black and yellow dress to grab your attention and impress - The Queen Bee."

"It did get my attention. Keep the dress. You look a lot better in yellow then I do. It looks good on you."

I smiled back at her with humble appreciation, "Thank you."

"Good, the Queen Bee is officially dead now."

Chapter 29

TONI

In the world of female wrestling there are big names like WWE, WOW and then there's my organization, the AWWL. The American Women's Wrestling League.

My name is Toni D'Angelo and I've owned this club for the past fifteen years.

My uncle Vinnie made a big investment when I first started it. I've managed to turn the AWWL into the number three female league in America.

In the beginning the AWWL was a member of the World Wrestling Alliance. It's an organization that regulates all leagues to make sure all the wrestling events put on are real and not faked.

Since my uncle was a big investor at the time, he insisted we be a member of the WWA.

As the years passed, my uncle became less involved with my company. When he finally let me run my league without his interference, I quit the WWA. I realized my company can make more money if we followed in the WWE and other sports entertainment formats.

Here we are, fifteen years after I started AWWL and my uncle isn't as involved as he used to be since my club is a huge success now. I still talk to him from time to time. He likes to make sure his investment is profitable. However, he doesn't know I quit the WWA because he has a lot of other businesses to run.

In a matter of speaking, he gave me the keys and lets me do what I want as long as I don't lose money.

My offices are located in New York City at the General Motors Building. The heart of everything that's important.

Today was a sunny day in the middle of the week, just before Labor Day weekend. I love sunny days in the big city. It makes this town feel alive.

Unexpectedly my assistant came rushing into my office, "Ma'am, you've got to see this!"

This was Veda Sato. A Japanese American girl who had short dark black hair, glasses, a small button nose and an ear bud in one ear. This hard-core nerd has been attached to my side for over six months.

She gets excited when she sees something on the internet that I need to take notice of.

I was slightly irritated by the way she barged in, "Veda, how many times have I told you not to charge in my office like that unless it's super important."

"I know, I'm sorry but I think you're going to want to see this."

Veda showed me a short video of a very tall female wrestler in the small-town of Fort Wayne, Indiana.

I've seen many tall wrestlers before. Most of them were men. Andre The Giant was over seven feet. Hulk Hogan was six-seven and there are many more. Too many to make a huge list of.

All the women who wrestle in the AWWL are between five-eight and six feet tall.

It is extremely rare to find a female that was as tall as the person in this video. I asked Veda, "Is this girl for real?"

She said, "If you're asking if the video is fake, as far as I can tell…no. It's not fake. I did a little digging and there was a small underground match in Fort Wayne a few days ago."

I watched this video repeatedly and wondered to myself, *"Can this be the same tall girl my brother Frank told me about not too long ago?"*

Veda told me, "Her name is The Queen Bee."

Then I shouted, "The Queen Bee! That's her!"

"Who?"

"My brother owns an underground strip club in the outskirts of Indianapolis, Indiana."

Veda cocked her head, "Wait, is that the one you told me about that was once a bouncer?"

"Yes! That's her. I told Frank to do mud and oil wrestling as a gimmick to get more customers in the door. He loved that idea. A few weeks later he sent me a video of Olivia mud wrestling."

"She went from bouncing to mud wrestling? Sounds like a step down."

I got my phone out and watched the video Frank sent me and compared it to Veda's video. "Look, they're the same person."

"Oh, that's too bad she's an ex-stripper."

"I don't know. She didn't act like a stripper and nobody is trying to do the typical - rip her top off in the mud - thing."

Veda gave me a look, "Ma'am, your top rule is no nudity. We don't want a situation like what happened before."

I handed her the tablet back, "Yeah, you're right."

"Sorry for the false alarm."

As Veda left my office, I pulled up the same video she showed me on YouTube. I watched it a few more times and then looked at the mud wrestling video Frank sent me on my phone.

The giant ass woman kicked ass in the mud.

My brain did its thinking out loud, "I really hope I don't find any nude pics of you on the internet. You could be my next huge star!"

Then I watched the video from Fort Wayne again. That same power but without the mess, "Wow, I need to keep an eye on you."

If I was a cartoon, you would have seen dollar signs in my eyeballs.

ABOUT THE AUTHOR

Frank James Bailey is a voice actor, writer and the creator of the Tercona comic book series. He also works as a security guard. He lives with his wife and two kids in the Lima, OH area.

Since 2015 he's dedicated his life to building the world of Tercona. He hopes to turn it into an animated series someday. If you want to know more about Tercona go to www.Tercona.com.

In 2023 he published his first romantic comedy novel called The Taming of April.

Now it's 2024 and this book is the first of a 3-book series about a very tall female wrestler.

He's still writing the Tercona comics. Look for comic #8 soon.

Frank now hopes to broaden his horizons and be more versatile with new and different stories.

www.ingramcontent.com/pod-product-compliance
Lightning Source LLC
Chambersburg PA
CBHW071513140726
47997CB00005B/1953